SENIORS GUIDE

TO

iPad

Yes! ☺

THE MOST COMPLETE AND INTUITIVE STEP-BY-STEP MANUAL

to Master your New iPad,

with Tips and Tricks for

Senior Beginner Users

TABLE OF CONTENTS

CHAPTER 3:
Network And Communication......48

CHAPTER 4: iPad Camera..........67

CHAPTER 12:

CHAPTER 13:

INTRODUCTION

On January 27, 2010, Steve Jobs, the founder and the then CEO of Apple, announced the "iPad" at an Apple press conference in San Francisco. The announcement of the iPad is a milestone in modern technology due to the versatility and portability it provides for consumers. Steve Jobs was always fascinated by computers, and he was always irked by the fact that tablets are less efficient when compared to modern computers.

From 1990 onwards, Jobs started to advance Apple's technology with the goal of making it usable by hand and capable of providing a great and unique experience to the end-user. Newton MessagePad, PowerBook Duo, and MessagePad 2100 are some of the early pioneers of the iPad which didn't gather much public attention. They were discontinued shortly after their respective launches due to lack of sales, and forced Steve Jobs to end his experimentation with tablets for a short period of time.

However, the future of a brand new Apple tablet became possible when in 2007 Steve Jobs announced a modern new device called the "iPhone" to the world. The iPhone also introduced a touch screen, which was a game-changer in the technological world back then.

With the massive success of the iPhone in 2007, Steve Jobs acquired enough capital for his ideas related to tablets to turn into an actual product, and by 2009, rumors had started to spread about Apple's new tablet all over public forums on the internet. The hype was real. People were delighted and excited by the fact that their tablet could serve as a reading, entertainment, and communication machine, and could sit right in their palms.

The iPad as a digital product has been successful right from its announcement. In less than 90 days of their availability, Apple sold more than three million iPads. There were always long queues of people in front of Apple stores to get hold of this next technology innovation that would later on become one of the most popular portable tablets in history.

By the launch of the next generation iPad 2, Apple had sold more than 15 million iPads, making it more popular than all other tablets available in the market. From their inception to now iPads have not lost their charm, but they have increased their advancements in technology and became a great portable device for multiple demographics. Modern iPads have a ton of uses and are visually appealing. The iPad research team at Apple has ensured that they provide value to as many people as possible.

iPad Model's History

For a decade Apple announced many models of the iPad to targeted customers from different demographics.

While it started as a single device model for all demographics a decade back, in 2022 Apple has different tiers of models available for customers of different demographics and for customers with different use cases.

1. Apple iPad (2010)

Announced in January of 2010, this is the first of the iPad line, and it came with an aluminum build and a 9.7-inch display.
Along with the A4 processor, the consumers had a chance to choose either a 32GB or 64GB variant.

2. Apple iPad 2 (2011)

The second-generation iPad was unveiled in 2011 with an A5 processor and practically improved in every area from the first-generation iPad.
iPad 2 was also released with front and back cameras, making it an excellent FaceTime supported video calling device.

3. Apple iPad 3 and Apple iPad 4 (2012)

The third-generation iPad released in 2012 had an A5X processor and boasted the inclusion of a retina display that offered four times more pixels than the previous generation iPads.

iPad 3 came with iOS6 and provided more stability to more than 200,000 applications that are available in the App Store.

Within just a few months, Apple's iPad 4 was released with an A6X processor that is way faster than the previous versions. iPad4 also started supporting dual-band Wi-Fi for more immediate and faster internet access.

4. Apple iPad Mini (2012)

For the first time, Apple launched the iPad Mini series along with the iPad 4 in 2012. iPad mini was significantly smaller than the regular iPad versions but offered the same operating system and efficiency for the user.

However, the Mini version doesn't have a Retina display but comes with a 1024x768 pixels HD display.

5. Apple iPad Air (2013)

iPad Air is a fifth-generation iPad model with a new A7 chip and 20% faster system processing. For the first time, iPad's boosted their ability to higher video frame rates and became a better option for professionals.

Apple also spent quality time reducing the bezels around this model, making it a better entertainment device.

6. Apple iPad Mini 2 (2013)

In the next release of the iPad mini version in 2013, Apple focused on improving the display resolution and included a much faster A7 chip on the device.

Even though the design remained the same, it did perform two times better than the Android tablets of the same size.

7. Apple iPad Air 2 (2014)

The second-generation iPad models had the slimmest design making them the best-looking tablets, and Apple also upgraded the chip to A8X. The significant change from the two Air models is the inclusion of Touch ID in the second generation Air model.

8. Apple iPad Mini 3 & 4 (2014-2015)

Both iPad Mini 3 and 4 had minor upgrades, and both had faster A8 processors and included a fully laminated display. Both front and back camera resolutions are also updated. However, Apple decided to stop Mini models after the iPad mini 4 temporarily.

9. Apple iPad Pro 12.9 and 9.7 (2015)

Apple iPad Pro is the iPad lineup that changed the potential of iPads and made sure that the iPads are no less than desktops and laptops in terms of efficiency. First-generation Pros were released in two sizes, 12.9 and 9.7 inches. They are also slimmer with a metal build. Along with iPad Pros, a new stylus called Apple Pencil was introduced in the Apple ecosystem. The significant advantage of the iPad Pro is its beautiful Retina display with more pixels and blazing fast refresh rate. iPad Pros are the best available devices available for professionals in the tablet market.

10. Apple iPad (2017—2021)

Even with the success of the Apple iPad Pro, Apple didn't completely ignore the low-end iPad models that sell well and cover a lot of demographics such as students and regular users. The basic Apple iPad is the cheapest tablet that Apple has offered its users for the past few years.

All the basic iPad versions had a previous generation Apple Silicon chip that works more than three times better than the Android tablets. Also, practically all different iPad versions run the same operating system, iPad OS. Basic iPad is also supported by Apple Pencil and Apple Keyboard.

11. Newer Apple iPad Pros (2017—2020)

All newer iPad Pro models are the best in the tablets right now. Apple ditched

Touch Id for the Pro models and included face ID for faster access.
With the latest Apple iPad Pro version running an A14 processor, it is as fast as a mac running with an Intel processor. Apple has also focused on increasing the refresh rate and provides a beautiful OLED-like screen for better saturation and brightness. These iPad Pros also support the second-generation Apple Pencil, which is a much better stylus than the first generation Apple Pencil.
All these Apple iPad Pro versions also come in different sizes.

12. All new iPad Air (2020)

Apple also provides a mid-tier Air choice for professionals who don't need a high-quality screen. iPad Air comes with a slim design along with a blazing A14 processor. It also uses USB-C charging, making it an excellent device for long-term usage.

13. Apple iPad with M1 processor (2021)

The newer iPad Pro version comes with an inbuilt M1 processor that is included in all Apple latest Macs. The M1 processor is six times faster than the Android tablets and three times faster than the Apple A14 processor.
The newer Apple iPad Pro also supports high-level augmented reality applications and the efficiency to render complex machine learning models. It is the best Apple can offer to its users in the present moment.

What's This Book?

This book is a tool to help seniors understand the basic functionalities of an iPad by using easy-to-understand explanations. Sometimes technology can be complicated for people due to different reasons. However, with a good guide, you can conquer your fears and experience the technology's advantages.

The iPad is a kind of technology that has a learning curve, but once you get the hang of it, there is a lot you can do.

The book's author has made sure that the seniors for whom this book is intended can understand the flow and the essence of the topics mentioned.

Whenever required, example scenarios and step-by-step instructions are provided for the reader.

How to Get the Most Out of This Book?

As a prerequisite, all you need is an iPad model of your preference and a strong will to learn to get the most out of this book. We also recommend you have an email account and a mobile number for Apple ID verification that sometimes needs to be done to operate the device.

To easily remember the steps or details mentioned in this book, we recommend you practically recreate every step on your own on your iPad for efficiently operating the system.

If you are confused, you can create a simple mind map or use passive recall techniques such as memory palace to remember the steps as it is.

Memory palace is a cognitive learning technique where readers can use their real-life locations to link with the concepts they want to remember.

Teaching someone unaware of the iPad operation about what you have learned can also be a great way to get used to the process.

Most Used Terminology in This Book

Even though this is a book written for laymans unaware of the Apple iPad, we still want you to understand some simple terminology included in this book to better understand the content provided.

1. Apple Ecosystem - Apple is an American company that provides different services and devices to its users. Apple made sure that you can access other Apple devices simultaneously and almost instantly with the help of their well-integrated ecosystem. For example, you can send files from your iPad to iPhone within a split second. Sticking to an ecosystem has both pros and cons.

2. Hardware - Hardware is the stuff that runs your iPad like it is intended to. Processor, screen, buttons, metal body, and speakers are some of the hardware components present in an iPad.

3. Operating System (OS) - Operating systems act as a communication between the user and the device. iPad uses iPad OS as the default operating system, and users can install no other operating system on an iPad.

4. App Store - iPad comes with several default apps, but you can install many more apps using the App Store. Imagine it like a shopping mall for your iPad, to buy and install different applications (apps). There are both paid and free apps in the App Store. At present, there are more than 2 million applications on the App Store.

5. Application - An application is a kind of software for a mobile or a portable device. For example, Maps installed on your iPad can be called an application. Different applications have different purposes.

6. iCloud - iCloud is the default cloud manager Apple provides for its users. With iCloud, you can store your images, videos, documents, and Appdata on the Apple cloud servers without fear of losing them ever again. If you have multiple devices, it becomes easy to sync the data with the help of iCloud. We will talk about how iCloud works in the latter chapters of the book.

7. Browser - A browser is software with which you can browse the world wide web. Safari is the default browser on the iPad, and you can also install third-party browsers such as Google Chrome and Firefox using the App Store.

8. Apple ID - Apple ID is the default ID that Apple asks you to access different Apple services such as iCloud. Without Apple ID, it is practically impossible to get the most out of your iPad.

9. Siri - Siri is the default voice application used by all Apple devices. With Siri, you can easily control your iPad with just voice commands.

10. Storage - All iPads come with fixed default storage to store your applications, multimedia files, and application data. You can also use iCloud storage along with the default storage to satisfy your storage needs while using an iPad.

11. Home screen - Your home screen is the equivalent to your desktop on your home computer. When you restart your device or touch your iPad touch ID button, your device will open to the home screen.

12. Wi-Fi/Cellular - iPads come in two different variants, known as Wi-Fi and cellular versions, based on internet connectivity. With Wi-Fi iPads, you can only connect to a Wi-Fi network, whereas with a cellular version, you can also connect to your iPad using mobile data.

What's Next?

Learning new technology is often challenging and overwhelming.

But with a comprehensive guide like this, you can become a pro with the device.

Remember to follow the instructions and carefully practice them to understand different operations better.

Let us dive into the comprehensive iPad guide now.

CHAPTER 1:
Introduction to iPad

iPad is one of the more popular technology devices that has revolutionized itself in the past 10 years.

With an iPad, you can read books, watch music, play videos, do office work, or make it a gaming machine with just a few clicks. Whenever an iPad gets released, you might have already seen the vast queues outside the Apple store. There is always a demand for iPads. Especially in the lockdown, Apple has reported selling three times more devices than they did the year before.

Buying an iPad can be an overwhelming decision because a lot of money needs to be invested, and there are a lot of iPads right now on sale, making it difficult for an individual to choose which one is best for them.

Which iPad to Choose?

Regardless of how many recommendations you look at, it would help if you ultimately decided on an iPad that serves your needs. Different iPad models have different purposes and target different demographics of customers. Remember that even though all these models differ from a hardware perspective, all run the same iPad OS.

So, you need not worry about incompatible apps when running a low-end iPad. However, it is important to understand that the Pro models provide some additional software enhancements to device owners.

Before buying an iPad, you need to judge your needs based on four criteria.

Display

One major factor that decides which iPad you are going to buy is the iPad's display. All iPad Pro models provide better quality screens in the industry, making them a better choice for professionals and for people who are attracted to visual appeal. Next-generation iPad Air models also offer great displays except for the Pro-motion technology that is exclusive for pro models. iPad Mini typically comes with the same Liquid Retina display present in the iPad Air models but with smaller screen sizes.
Basic iPad models have a lot less resolution, brightness and are not provided with a laminated display. However, they still come with an excellent retina display for their price point.

While obviously leaving which iPad model to choose entirely to your choice, we still want to provide recommendations for you.

- **iPad Pro models** - Best for digital artists, professionals, and people who need better visual contrast
- **iPad Air models** - Best for everyone
- **iPad Mini models** - Best for people who love small screens
- **Basic iPad** - Best for light users

If You Want to Choose an iPad Based on Screen Size

- **12.9-inch screens** - For people who can't see the text correctly on small screens
- **10.9-inch screens** - Best for all users
- **8.3-inch screens** - Best for people who get uncomfortable with large text

If You Want to Choose an iPad Based on Usage

- **Digital Drawings and Media Consumption** - iPad Pro models
- **Light usage** - Basic iPad model
- **Reading** - iPad mini

If you are someone with visual impairment, it is recommended to use either iPad Pro or iPad Air models. They come with a wide color display, making it easy for you to interact with the screens without stressing much on your eyes.

Processing Power

Processing power is another critical factor you need to consider before purchasing an iPad.

All new iPad models, irrespective of price, can handle complex tasks.

However, if you are a user who needs high graphical power and needs an advanced Neural engine, then the new iPad Pro model that comes with an Apple M1 chip is the best choice for you.

Newer iPad Pro models can also be bought with either 8 Gigabytes (GB) RAM or 16GB RAM.

Before buying an iPad, you need to judge your needs based on four criteria.

If You Want to Choose an iPad Based on Usage

- **Light user** - iPad Basic model (6th generation and above)
- **Complex tasks** - iPad Pro models and iPad mini

Storage

Many users nowadays depend on cloud storage to meet their storage needs. However, if you are an iPad user who needs a lot of storage, choosing pro models is a better option because you can get storage up to 2 Terabytes (TB) with the newer iPad Pro models. Basic iPads start with 64 GB making them insufficient for many users.

If You Want to Choose an iPad Based on Storage Requirement

- **iPad Pro models** - For people with a memory requirement of more than 256 GB
- **iPad Air models** - For people with a memory requirement of more than 64 GB and less than 256 GB
- **iPad Basic models** - For light users with less memory requirement

Network Connection

All iPad models come with two different variants based on network communication.

1. Wi-Fi models are great for people who stay indoors most of the time and don't need to travel a lot.
2. Wi-Fi+Cellular models are great for people who travel a lot with their devices.

Once you have decided which iPad to choose, reach out to your nearest Apple store or order from the official website. Several payment options such as Apple Pay, Google Pay, credit, and debit cards are available for ordering an iPad of your choice either on the website or in the store.

Explore What's in the Box

Once you buy your iPad, the package will be delivered to you in one beautifully-packaged box. Apple uses minimal packaging that looks aesthetic.
Once you open the box, you will see the below items for any iPad model.

• iPad
First, you will see the iPad itself in the package box. The iPad will usually be covered in a thick plastic sleeve that you can take off. Ensure not to throw it away, as it is essential to have it if you want to return the iPad for a replacement within 14 days.

• Documentation
You will see the next set, a small instruction handbook that displays the essential things to start using an iPad. It is not comprehensive but can help you power on/off for the first time and help you understand the Button layout that exists in your iPad version. You will also receive premium Apple stickers for your purchase.

• A USB-C or Lightning-to-USB cable
A USB cord is essential for connecting your iPad to a computer or for the USB power adapter. Higher-end iPad models come with the faster USB-C cord, whereas the basic models use lightning cable.

• USB power adapter
A power adapter helps you connect your iPad to a power source for charging. All newer iPad power adapters usually come with faster-charging abilities. These are the only things that you will be able to find in your package box, along with a warranty slip for your device.

Note:
To confirm that your iPad is legit, make sure to reconfirm your IMEI number on

the official website. To check your IMEI number, click *#06# on your keypad if it's an iPad with cellular options. If you are using a Wi-Fi model, then make sure to check the serial number from the settings panel to verify that your iPad is brand new.

First Look at Your iPad

At first glance, you will be amazed by the design and build of the iPad that you are holding in your hands. Different iPad models have different designs and buttons, and it is essential to know the basic details of your iPad model to confirm that you have received the suitable model.

Here is a rundown of some of the hardware features iPads are included with.

• Home/Touch ID
The home button and Touch ID are the same but work efficiently for two different purposes. Touch ID is usually used to unlock your device with your fingerprint quickly. The home button, when pressed, can also take you back to the home screen from any application. Double-clicking on the home button will also show a list of open apps right now. You can use this scrolling list of apps to move from one app to another without ending them quickly. In the newer Pro and Air models, the Home button is not present, and to get this scrolling list of apps, hand swiping gestures are used.

• Sleep/Wake button
Typically you can use this button to let the device power on, sleep or wake it up from sleep.

• Lightning / USB-C connector

You can use this slot to charge your device. You can either connect to the power adapter or the computer to charge your device. When connected to a computer using these slots, your device files will also be synced with the computer.

• Smart Connector

This connector will help you connect your device to unique accessories such as Keyboard and Apple Pencil.

• Speakers

The iPad has great stereo speakers that support Dolby Atmos and Spatial audio. While iPad basic and Air models provide two speakers, Pro models come with four speakers, giving the best sound among all.

• Volume buttons

The volume switches, also known as a rocker, can increase or decrease the volume. You can also use this button to Zoom in and out your web pages in full-screen mode.

• Headphone jack and microphone

Unlike iPhones, there is also a headphone jack of 3.5mm for iPad users. You can use this jack to listen to music using headphones.
There is also a microphone for the device to detect your voice commands given to Siri or while making voice/ video calls using social media and messaging applications.

• Cameras

All iPads have both front and rear-facing cameras for you to take pictures, make conference calls or shoot movies.
All the newer iPad Pro models have Lidar sensors that can help you use more robust augmented reality apps.

We will be discussing the physical hardware specifications of the newer popular models to help you quickly verify your device.

1. iPad Pro models (3rd generation and newer)

All iPad pro newer models come with two screen sizes of 12.9 inches and 10.9 inches. There will be no home button on these models, making it a unique design choice in iPad models. To switch on the iPad, you need to use the "Top" button. Along with the Top button, there are two volume buttons on the device. You will also see a front camera and rear cameras at the back. All iPad Pro models use Face ID to unlock the device. If yours is a Wi-Fi + cellular model, there will be a SIM tray. You will also see a USB-C connector at the bottom of the device. On the left corner of the iPad Pro, you can also see a magnetic connector used to attach Apple Pencils.

2. iPad Air (4th generation)

The newer iPad Air model also doesn't have a home button, but a Touch ID is present at the top of the device. Your iPad can be unlocked using the Touch ID. Apart from this, all other physical specifications are similar to iPad Pro models.

3. iPad (from 5th generation to 9th generation)

The basic iPad models all have a home button with a Touch ID and a top button, and volume buttons are also present on the side. All basic iPad models use a lightning port to charge the device. You can also find a SIM tray for a cellular model.

4. iPad Mini models

The newer iPad models have only the top button, whereas the older ones have a Touch ID with a home button. You can easily recognize a mini model because it is minimal compared to other iPads. The newer mini models also have a magnetic connector to attach an Apple Pencil.

Once you verify the iPad, you are now all set to start the iPad for the first time. Carefully follow the below-mentioned instructions to set up your iPad correctly.

Starting Your iPad for the First Time

To ensure that the iPad setup is done as intended, you need to ensure that the following items are available.

- A working network connection (Wi-Fi or cellular) is available
- Apple ID and password
- Any credit or debit card information to add payment information
- Any backup if it is available
- Any old device that you are trying to migrate data from

Once all the prerequisites are available, Press and hold the Top button of your iPad for a few seconds until the Apple logo appears. If it didn't start, make sure to charge it for at least 30 minutes before performing the same task.

Once the iPad starts, you will be welcomed with a welcome message. When you see this message, either press the home button or swipe up if you are using an iPad Pro model for the initial setup to begin.

1. **Choose the language** of your choice.
2. **Choose your country** or region.
3. **In the following interface, if you want to set up your iPad from scratch, click on the "Set up Manually" button**. If not, you can bring your other iPad or iPhone close to your device for it to recognize your saved settings and setup automatically.
4. **Choose a Wi-Fi network for the procedure to begin if you have a Wi-Fi-only model.** If you have a cellular model, then you may have to select your mobile network during this process.
5. **Once your Wi-Fi is connected, your iPad will connect to the iPad server and verify your hardware information.** Once connected, you may need to look

at the data & privacy policy Apple follows. Click on "Continue" to proceed to the next interface.

6. **In the next section, you may need to create a Touch ID or Face ID depending on your iPad model.** If it is Touch ID, you should place your thumb on the home button several times, as mentioned on the screen. If it is Face ID, you should look at the device camera and turn your face according to the onscreen instructions. You can always choose "Set up later" to add these authentication features later in the Settings menu.

7. **After creating a Touch ID and Face ID, you may also need to add a passcode for the device.** Adding a passcode provides additional encryption features for your device. Also, every time you reboot your device, it is mandatory to enter a passcode even though you have Touch ID/Face ID configured. You have to enter a passcode and renter it to verify your code and proceed to the next interface.

8. **In the "Apps & Data" setup page, you will be able to restore apps from an iCloud backup or by using Mac or PC.** If you are setting up for the first time, click on the "Don't transfer apps & data" option.

9. **In the following interface, the device will ask you to authenticate with your Apple ID and password.** While it is not mandatory to log in at this point, you, however, need an Apple ID in the future to access any Apple services such as iCloud, Apple Music, or Apple TV. If you have entered the Apple ID, you may need to enter a two-factor authentication code sent to your other devices or mobile number. Once done, click on the "Agree" button to accept Apple IDs terms and conditions.

10. **You will now be asked to update your iPad if there are any newer versions.** Usually, the iPad will come with the latest version installed, so click on the "Continue" button.

11. **You can add any card details you want to use on your iPad for Apple pay purchases**. If not, click on the "Set up later" button.

12. **You can now set up your iCloud Keychain related to your passwords in this interface.** We highly suggest you click on 'continue' for efficiently transferring any sensitive information from other devices.

13. **In the following interface, you need to install Siri for your device.** Just follow the onscreen instructions and say the commands that are displayed on the screen for Siri to take note of your voice and respond in future.

14. **In the next interfaces, you can start screen time features or decide whether or not to provide app analytics for the developers.** If you are confused, skip all the steps as you can set all these settings later on your device easily.

15. **In the last setup process, select whether you want light mode or dark mode for your device.**

Within a few seconds, a few tabs will show up, explaining some basic information about dock, access controls, and recent apps. Just click "Continue" on all of them for the "Welcome to iPad" message to show up. When you see this pop-up message on the screen, tap on "Get Started" for you to be taken into the iPad home screen for the first time.

Understanding Multi-Touch Screen Gestures

The first time you see your iPad home screen, you will see a few icons and a pretty background. A dock will appear just like in mac with all critical applications required for a better iPad experience. You can first observe the icons, screen, and dock for some time to understand what the iPad has to offer for you.

Touch the screen carefully. All iPad screens are made of high-quality glass that is very strong compared to other electronic screens. You can also use screen protectors not to get scratches on any screen parts. iPad users usually use paper screen protectors as they will be using an Apple Pencil a lot of time.

As an iPad user, you need to use touchscreen technology to navigate your iPad. Usually, if you are unfamiliar with touchscreens, it may seem overwhelming at first to navigate the device. Learning some of the primary touch screen gestures can help you efficiently perform tasks on your iPad.

To warm yourself up with the device, perform the below-mentioned task on your iPad:

• Go to the home screen and search for the "Settings" app icon. When you find it, tap on it and observe what happens.

• When you are in the Settings interface, tap on the Home button or swipe up from the bottom to be taken to the home screen again.

• Swipe your finger from left to right or right to left on the home screen to move between different screens. Observe the white dots present on the home screen to understand what screen you are on.

• Turn your iPad sideways or into landscape mode to observe how the screen rotation works.

• Drag your finger from the top of the screen to the edge in the middle for the notification center to unveil. You can also drag your finger from the top edge of the screen to the bottom for the control center to unveil.

Important Touch Screen Gestures

1. Tap once
This will be your most used touch screen out of the lot. Tapping once lets the

the screen recognize your input.

For example:

- You can tap one of the app icons to open your applications.
- You can tap once on links to head over to a web page.
- You can tap once on a song to play it.
- You can tap once on a checklist to quickly mark it or unmark it.

2. Tap Twice & Pinch
You can easily zoom in or out of web pages using the tap twice method. You can also use this method while in the Maps app to zoom in or zoom out of the street view quickly. The pinch can be used as an alternative method for tapping twice. You can pinch your fingers together to quickly zoom in or zoom out of any web page, map, or application in pinch mode.

3. Swiping
When you touch the screen and move either left or right to turn web pages or pages in an ebook, it is called swiping. Swiping is very common in all native and third-party applications. You can practice swiping by heading over to the home screen and moving from one screen to another by moving with your fingers.

4. Flick
The flick gesture can be used to move as fast you can to the bottom or top of a web page. In a flick gesture, the user should usually flick the finger in the direction they want to move.

5. Tap on the status bar
When you tap on the status bar while in any part of the web page, you will be immediately taken to the top of the page. Not all sites support this feature, and sometimes you need to double-tap on the status bar to function.

6. Press and hold

With iOS13, iPad OS has a drag and drop function for all iPads. You can hold the item and move it along to place it elsewhere in any app that supports drag and drop. For example, you can press the text on a web page to hold it and drag it into a notes app.

The Dock

Dock helps iPad users easily select and open their favorite or most-used apps.

A dock is often divided by a gray line.
All the icons on the left side of this gray line are the apps you use most often.

On the other hand, icons to the right are the suggestions provided by iPad for its users based on your usage performance.

You can also easily reorder or remove apps from the dock by tapping and holding the icons onto your screen.

Onscreen Keyboard

While using any application, you need to make sure that you know the complete functionalities an onscreen keyboard provides.
Using landscape mode while typing on the onscreen keyboard is recommended for a better typing experience on your iPad.

What does your onscreen keyboard contain?

● An emoji bar where you can select any emoji while messaging or while posting on the internet.

● A globe icon that helps you to change different keyboard settings. You can easily change the language or style that you want for your keyboard from here.

● You can use the delete key to delete any text with just a single tap. You can also hold and select all the text you want to delete and click on this button for faster deletion.

● You can click on the "Return" button to create a new paragraph.

● Double tapping shift can make you turn on Caps Lock on the iPad. A single tap, however, can turn it off.

● You can also choose different symbols present on the onscreen keyboard using the shift menu.

● By clicking on the button that looks like a voice recorder on the keyboard, you can dictate text onto your keyboard.

If you feel uncomfortable using an onscreen keyboard, you can attach other accessories such as Magic Keyboard and Smart Keyboard folio to your iPad.

Flick to Search

With a flick on your iPad, you can effortlessly search for different suggestions related to your device. To open a suggestions panel on your home screen, swipe down any area of your home screen apart from the edges.

You will immediately see a search pop-up that has a text field. Enter any query to find results. Use the scroll down option to quickly look at different results and tap on them to open in an appropriate app or player.

Switch Between Apps

Switching between apps makes it easy to have a multitasking experience on your iPad. When your apps run in the background, they will not end their app lifecycle but will stay there in the form where you left them to be.

You can switch between apps in two different ways:

1. Click on the home screen twice to open the app switcher; or,

2. If there is no home screen on your iPad, then you can swipe up from the bottom edge of the screen to display an app switch.

Users can use swipe actions to preview different open apps when on an App Switcher. Now, just clicking on any app can make the switch happen.

Slide Over

Slide over is a new iPad OS feature introduced in iPad OS13 for all iPad models. Slide over design was made to increase productivity for iPad users. In a slide over feature, a floating panel will be raised and can be slid over on the top of your app.

How to Start a Slide Over :

• Open an app and swipe from the bottom edge on a landscape or portrait mode for the dock to open.

• Now in the dock, touch any app of your choice and hold for it a few moments.

• After holding, you can try to drag it to the above app for the app to slide over onto your first app.

• You can click on your home screen or swap up from the bottom of your screen to end the slide over session.

Slide over can be beneficial when you browse the web while taking quick notes to your notes app.

Split View

Split view is an iPad feature where you can multitask on two apps for a more extended period. However, remember that not all apps support split mode.

The developer needs to code the split mode explicitly, and hence for the apps restricted to portrait mode, split-screen is not possible for now.

Initially split view used to work only for landscape mode, but from iPad OS15 on, Apple has provided a way to run portrait applications.

How to Enter a Split View :

• Open an app and swipe from the bottom edge.

• Open an app and swipe from the bottom for the dock to open. Now select an application from the document and drag it to the left or right of the application screen.

• Your app will now be ready to be split into the screen. A gray line appears between the two apps. You can use this to increase or decrease your split-screen size.

• You can drag any of the applications to the farthest for the split-screen mode to end.

Control Center

Control center is an exclusive Apple devices feature that helps users easily interact with different system components without worrying about the various complexities that the settings menu may usually provide.

How to Use the Control Center?

1. To use the control center, you need to swipe down from the upper right corner of the screen.

2. In the control center, you can use holding and swiping or tapping options to control them.

3. Once you have changed the settings from the control center, you can exit it by tapping on any part of the screen.

You can go to Settings > Control Center and add or remove different controls from the menu.

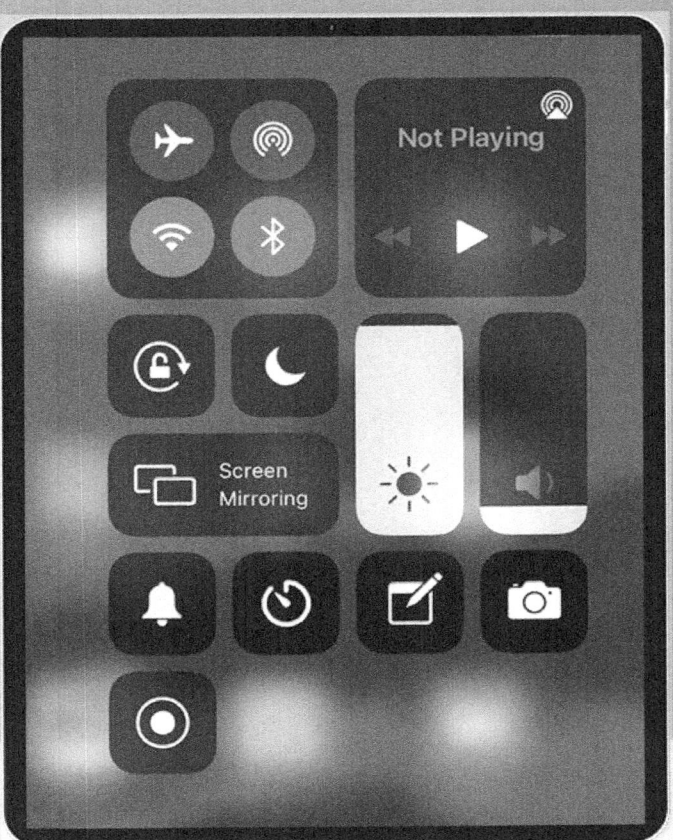

Status Bar

The status bar helps iPad users quickly know some of the essential details about their device.

These status bar icons change according to the iPad model you are using.

For example, a cellular iPad will display both mobile network and Wi-Fi on the status bar, whereas Wi-Fi only the iPad displays only Wi-Fi network on the status bar.

What are some of the icons?

- A Wi-Fi signal

- A mobile network signal

- A battery icon with the percentage

- Any icons that represent the tasks that you are currently running

- Time

- Do not Disturb icon

- Screen rotation lock

17:08 Tue 8 Mar   🔋 20% ⚡

CHAPTER 2:
iPad App Store & Apps

For getting the most out of any new technological device, you must have a working email address. Apple ID is mandatory for using all Apple services and requires an email address to start functioning.

Create a GMail Account

While many email services are available, GMail is the most popular one.
It is offered by Google and is easy to create.

● Head over to www.gmail.com and click on "Sign Up" to create your own account.

● Enter the email address you want to choose along with a strong password.

● You will get a verification code for the mobile number you have entered. Once your mobile number is verified, your Google account will be created and can be used to create an Apple ID account.

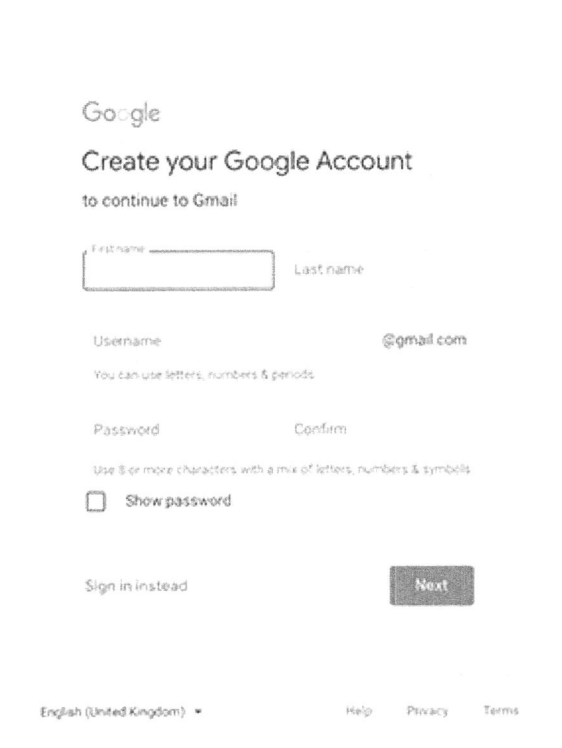

Create an Apple ID

Apple ID is one ID for all Apple's services that can be used on all Apple devices. Apple made it easy to create an Apple using different ways. You can use your iPad, iPhone, Mac, or even web browser to create a new Apple ID.

To create a new Apple ID on iPad, head over to your home screen and click on the App Store app.

• Once in the application, tap on the sign-in button and select "Create New Apple ID" from the pop-up.

• From now on, follow the on-screen instructions. Enter the email address you have to create before and other details such as name, location, mobile number, address, and billing details.

• In the next step, confirm the verification code sent to your phone number and email.

• After verification, you need to agree to the "Terms & Conditions" of Apple ID services by clicking on "Agree."

Within a few seconds, your account will go live, and you can now use Apple ID for services such as iCloud.

Installing Apps From the App Store

Once you have logged into your Apple Store and have reviewed your account, you will be all set to download apps and games to your device.

In the app store, you will be able to move between five tabs, and each provides a different use case for the user.

● "Today" is the first tab where Apple recommends different popular applications. Apple uses machine learning algorithms to suggest apps that you may like.

● "Games" is the second tab and helps you find the popular games on the iPad right now.

● "Apps" is the third tab that can help you to install different mobile applications onto your device directly.

● "Apple arcade" is the fourth tab in the application. It is a premium service that Apple provides for gamers on iOS devices.

● In the fifth tab, you are able to search millions of applications that are available on the App Store.

For every app preview present in the App Store, you can understand how an app will look on your device.

Other details such as file size, privacy information, and the description provided can help you choose from many similar apps.

The "Ratings & Reviews" section can also help individuals understand the authenticity and popularity of an application with other users in the ecosystem.

How to Download Apps

To download any app, first tap on the application from the provided list.

- Near the app icon, you will see a "Get" button for free applications. If it is a paid application, then the price for the application will appear there.

- Click on it for it to automatically be downloaded into your device.

- If it is a free application, you need to either enter your password or use Touch ID/ Face ID to provide your consent.

- On the other hand, if it is a paid application, you need to accept the payment pop-up that comes up.

There are a lot of applications for iPad OS that you can try out by yourself with the instructions provided above.

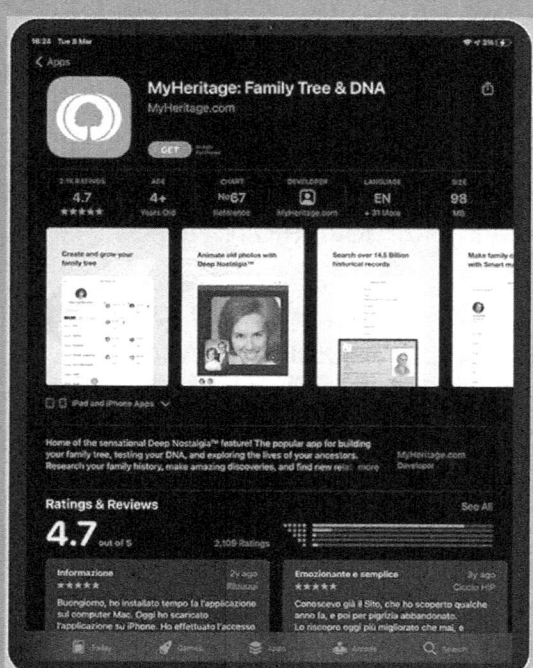

How to Remove Apps

To remove any app from your App Library, click and hold on to the app you want to delete. It will show a pop-up list. Select the "Delete app" option.

Note: When you delete the app, all the content will be deleted. So, confirm before deleting your app data.

Stock Apps

Several stock apps are installed automatically by Apple when you first boot your iPad. We will be discussing most of these apps in this book in the coming chapters. You must know the basic features of these apps for getting the most out of your device.

1. Books
This default reader application for iPad will help you read documents such as .pdf and .epub files. Apple Book Store, an inbuilt book application, allows people to buy ebooks and audiobooks on their iPad easily.

2. Calendar
Calendar is a default application that helps iPad users to create events for different dates seamlessly. It is a great organizational tool for iPad users.

3. Camera
Default camera application can make iPad users utilize the prowess of the high-quality camera provided for the users.

4. Clock
Default clock application make it easy for iPad users to look at the world clock and create alarms. It also provides additional features such as a stopwatch and timer, making it a great native application.

5. Contacts

This native application will help you store a lot of numbers of your friends, family, and colleagues in an organized way.

6. FaceTime

FaceTime is Apple's default video communication application for its users in the ecosystem.

7. Files

The Files app will help you easily manage and organize the data on your iPad. iCloud drives will also be displayed using this application.

8. Find My iPad

Find my iPad protects iPad from any theft. It is always recommended to switch this on to track your device easily.

9. Mail

The default mail application helps you to easily read or send mail using your iPad.

10. Maps

This native application will help you to look at maps and help you to easily go to a location with the help of GPS.

11. Music

This default application helps you to listen to music. The built-in music application can be linked with the Apple Music subscription service to listen to millions of songs on the go.

12. News

With this native application, iPad users can easily read news articles and magazines.

13. Messages

This is the native messaging platform for iOS devices. All your messages will be immediately synced to your other devices. You, however, can only message iOS users with this application.

14. Notes

The notes app can be used to write small quick notes or long manuscripts on your iPad. You can also scribble on the notes app using accessories such as an Apple Pencil.

15. Photos

This default application will help you to look at the photos that you have taken by your iPad camera or that you have saved to the iCloud or internal storage of your device. Photos app is also capable of playing video files.

16. Safari

Safari is the default browser for Apple devices. It is simple, fast, and tracks fewer data from the users when compared to other popular browsers such as Google Chrome.

There are many other native applications on the iPad, which we will be discussing in detail in the later chapters.

Popular Apps in Different Categories

Apple divides its apps into different categories such as: **utilities, productivity, social network,** and **games.** Knowing about some of the popular apps in different categories can help you get the most from your device.

Utility Apps

Utility apps are the apps that are used to make the device performance improve. Utility apps try to improve basic functionalities that sometimes native software can't provide.

Popular Utility Apps for iPad :

1. Google
This search app can help you easily search any query.

2. Evernote
Evernote is a popular note-taking app that can sync between different devices. Evernote also provides efficient annotation ability for the users.

3. SwiftKey Keyboard
Swiftkey replaces the default Apple iPad keyboard with a new and much more efficient keyboard. You can add more languages and get better auto-completion abilities with this software.

Productivity Apps

Productivity apps help you to do more work with less time. They can be used by both students and professionals to complete their tasks efficiently.

Popular Productivity Apps for iPad :

1. Ulysses
Ulysses is a popular writing app for iPad users. It is nicely-designed and

provides great features for organization abilities.

2. Todoist
Todoist helps you to become better at task management.

3. Session
Session is a Pomodoro timer app that helps iPad users easily track their productive time.

Social Networking Apps

Social networking apps help iPad users to easily network with their friends, colleagues, and family.
All these social network apps will work both on browsers and iPad.
However, iPad apps provide a better experience when compared to a web browser.

Popular Social Networking Apps :

1. Instagram
An image-sharing social network worldwide.

2. Facebook
A social media network that lets people easily connect with each other online.

3. TikTok
A video-sharing platform that has become a cultural phenomenon.

Games

iPads are never dedicated hand game consoles like a Nintendo Switch. However, Apple has constantly tried to provide better games for the average user. The recent inclusion of a game subscription plan known as "Apple Arcade" in their services has made sure that Apple is serious about providing a wonderful gaming experience to its users.
The game library is growing huge with every passing day.

Popular Games for iPad :

1. 2048
A fun mathematical puzzle game.

2. Fortnite
A battle royale game that is very popular worldwide.

3. Witness
A puzzle game with mind-bending puzzles and scenarios.
Apart from these, you can also install emulators such as Delta to play old retro games on your iPad.

Shopping Apps

E-commerce and online food ordering has become a necessity for many people now. **iPad provides a great library of apps for all of your shopping needs.**

Popular Shopping Apps :

1. Amazon
The official app for the largest e-commerce platform in the world.

2. Depop
A popular shopping platform for vintage and second-hand clothes.

3. Dominos Pizza
The official application for the Domino's Pizza outlets.

CHAPTER 3:
Network and Communication

Unlike 20 years ago, the world is now connected like a spiderweb with the help of the internet. The internet is also filled with websites that help people do practically anything they want. You can order a dress or watch an old movie or play a game with your buddies with the help of the internet.

iPad, as a device, is capable of doing countless things that the internet offers for the users. **Learn about some of the different ways to use the web and communicate with your loved ones or acquaintances using the basics covered for you in this chapter.**

How Will Your iPad Access the Internet?

iPad uses its Wi-Fi or cellular capability to connect to the internet.
Even when you are first setting up your device, an internet connection is mandatory for Apple to check the authenticity of your device. So, if you don't have Wi-Fi or a mobile data-enabled device, then your device will not start functioning as intended.

What Is Wi-Fi?

Wi-Fi is a network facility that helps devices connect to the network wirelessly.

All you need is a Wi-Fi connection from your nearby network service provider and a router to use Wi-Fi for several devices such as your smartphone, iPad, and computer. There are also many public hotspots worldwide that allow you to access the internet for free or for a nominal fee.

What Is Cellular Data?

Cellular data is a network facility where you can access the internet with the help of the SIM card or by an active mobile connection you are using on your device. iPad's with cellular data support usually cost more than the Wi-Fi-enabled iPads.

How to Connect to the Internet

To connect to the internet, **head over to Settings > Wi-Fi, or Settings > Mobile Data and connect to your home or mobile network.** To verify whether or not your network connection is active, you can open the App Store. If the App Store opens without any problems, your internet connection is active.

To get the most out of the internet, you need browsers to visit different websites. All modern browsers use complex frameworks to quickly parse web pages and provide them to the end-user intuitively.
Safari, the browser developed by Apple, is one of the smoothest and visually appealing browsers available right now for internet users. Safari is exclusive to Apple devices and a native app for iPad users.

How to Browse the Web

Browsing the web on Safari is fun as it has a great Graphical User Interface (GUI) and a lot of options for the users to get the most out of their web experience. You will see a list of icons and text fields on the browser on the top of the screen, and each of them has a specific functionality.

- The icon that looks like a book is used to expand the Safari settings and tab details.

- The buttons that look like less than (<) and greater than (>) symbols both take you to the previous and next page.

- When you tap on the "aA" button, you will be able to enter into the reader view, or you can increase or decrease the font size of the web page text.

- In the text field you can enter the Uniform Resource Locator (URL)—web address—of the website you want to visit.

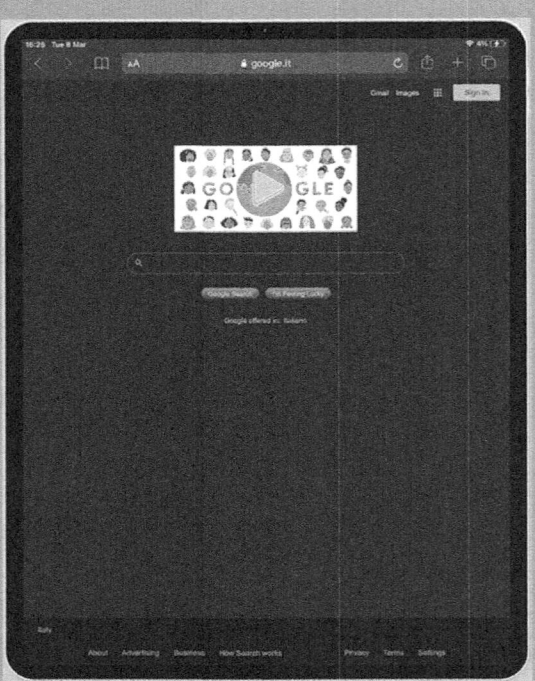

- The button that looks like a half-circle can be used to reload your webpage.

- With the share button that looks like a mail icon, you can easily share your web page link or add it to a bookmark list. There is also an option to print the page easily.

- When you click the "+" button, a new tab can be opened on the browser.

- The last icon with four boxes can help you to quickly shift between different tabs that are opened in your browser

You can change several settings for Safari according to your liking. Head over to Settings > Safari and change some of the settings mentioned below for better browsing abilities.

• Set the default search engine to Google as it is much better than its rivals (such as Bing).

• Toggle on the "Block Pop-ups" option to block any pop-ups while browsing the web.

• Verify or change the default file location for your website downloads.

• Click on the "Extensions" option to look at the extensions you have installed for Safari. You can easily search different extensions for Safari using the App Store.

• Toggle on the "Prevent Cross-site Tracking" option for additional encryption while browsing.

History

It is easy to track your browsing history with Safari, even if it is a month old. All your records will automatically be synced to your iCloud account, making it easy for you to go back into your recently-visited web pages from the other devices.

1. To view your recent history during the session, click and hold the previous page button to get recently-visited web pages. Just tap on them to see them.

2. To view your history more comprehensively, click on the top-left icon and tap on the "History" option. You will now be able to see your browsing history from more than a week before.

3. If you want to delete the history, click on the "Clear" button.

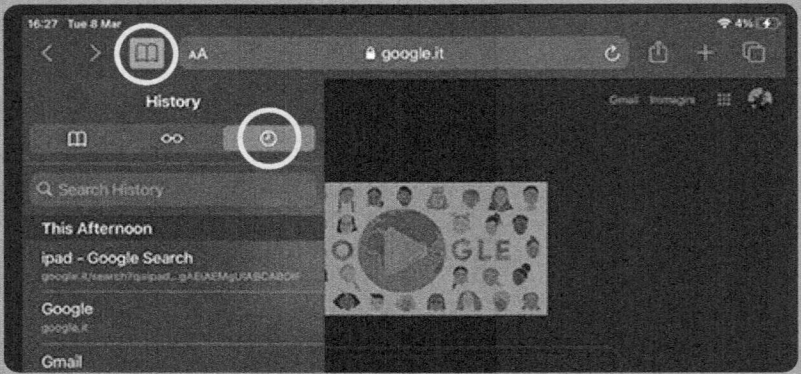

Search

Safari provides an inbuilt search feature for iPad users to make use of.
Usually, by default, Google is the default search engine for all iPad users.
Go to the address field and enter any search term for the browser to detect your queries and provide search suggestions.

If you are not satisfied with the search suggestions, click on the "Go" button present on the onscreen keyboard to open a Google search results page.

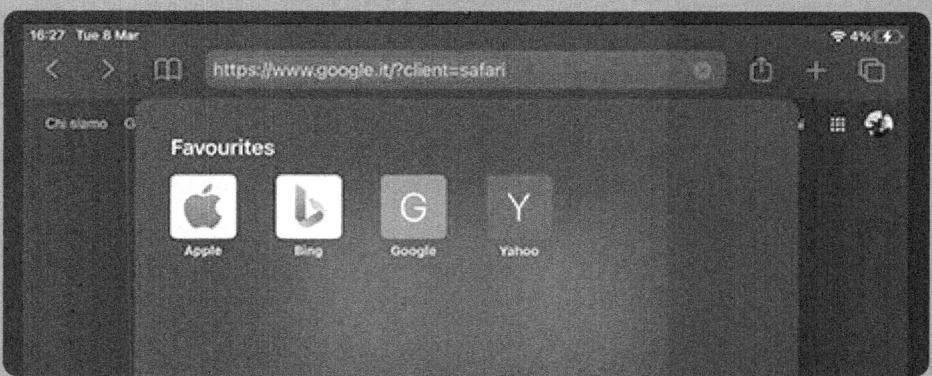

Bookmarks

Bookmarks act as an easy way to save your favorite web pages in your browser and visit them any way you want.

How to Create a Bookmark

• **To create a bookmark for any web page,** click on the share button that looks like an upward-pointing arrow on the browser. It will open a pop-up interface, where you need to click the "Add Bookmark" button.

• Immediately, you will be taken to another pop-up interface where you can edit the bookmark name for you to easily revisit it after. Once edited, click on the "Save" button to save the bookmark into your browser and iCloud.

• You can now click on the tab on the top left to visit your bookmarks any time you want to.

• You can also organize bookmarks into folders in this section.
There is also an option to delete bookmarks that you no longer need.

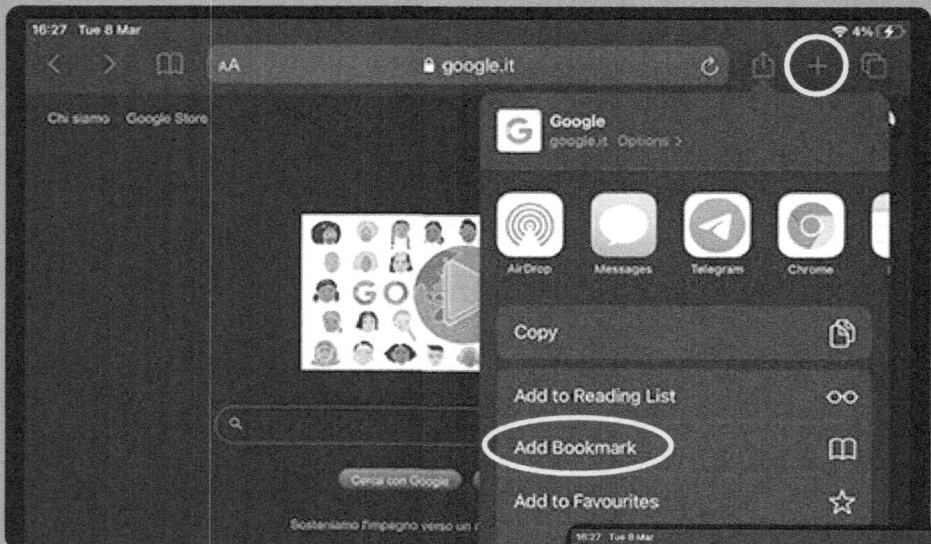

Apart from bookmarks, you can also use reading lists to save web pages temporarily.
Just click on the share button and click on the "Add to Reading list" button. After reading, you can mark the list item as "Read" for it to disappear from your reading list.

Private Browsing

Private browsing, also known as incognito mode, helps iPad users surf the web anonymously. While not to be confused with Virtual Private Networks (VPN), using the private browsing option doesn't stop your Internet Service Providers (ISPs) or governments from tracking you. Private browsing, however, makes sure that no cookies or log-in details are saved in the browser.

To start using private browsing, click on the "Show/Hide tab" icon on the top left screen, and click on the "Private Browsing" option. You can now click on the "+" button to open a new private tab. Remember that no search history will be saved when you are in private browsing mode.

Download Files

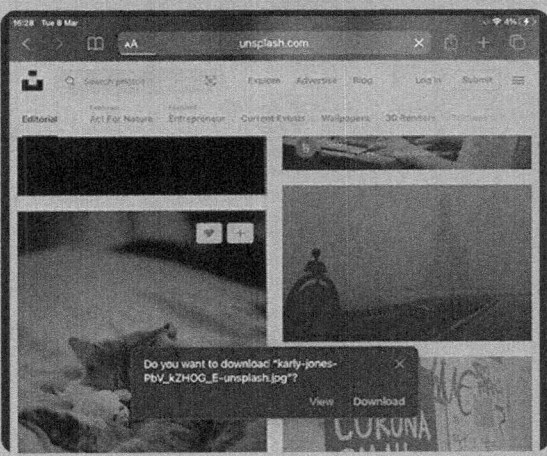

iPad OS13 made it easy for Safari users to download files into the iCloud and iPad file manager. First of all, head over to **Settings > Downloads** and choose a location that you want to use.

To download any files, you first have to click the link on the website, and the browser will automatically redirect a pop-up for you. **Click on the "Allow" button on the pop-up for the download to start.**

Link Preview

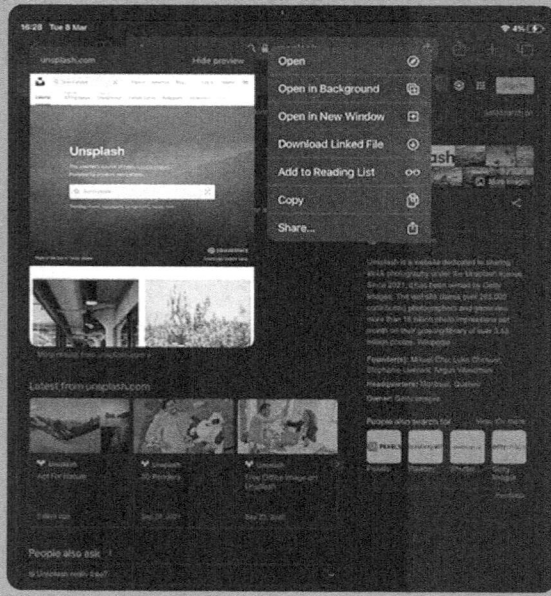

Apple makes it easy to preview any web page before clicking on it.

This feature can help you avoid spam pages that can load malware onto your device.

To preview a page, click and hold the link for a pop-up to arise where you can see a part of the web page.

Apart from these features, newer versions of Safari can also neglect any trackers that are present on websites

Contacts

Saving contacts is essential for accessible communication.
iPads provide a Contacts app for users to add, edit, or delete contacts in their device. All your contacts will be automatically synced to your iCloud account, making it easy for you to have the contact information on different devices almost instantly.

Tap on the Contacts app on the home screen to edit and personalize information.

How to Create a Contact

To create a new contact in your device, click on the "+" button on the screen when you first open the Contacts application.

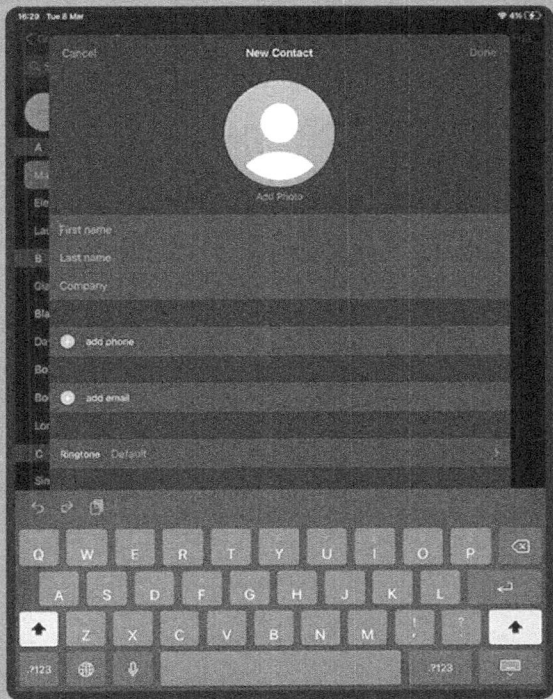

A pop-up will arise where you can add details such as first name, second name, company, phone number, email, social profiles, and other additional information for the contact. You can also add details about your relationship with the contact in the "related name" column. You can also add a photograph if you want to for the contact.

Once added, you can change the contact details anytime by tapping on the "Edit" button. However, you can also remove the contact's details by tapping on the "Delete" button that is present at the lower bottom of the screen.

FaceTime

FaceTime makes it easy for iPad users to stay in touch with their family and friends irrespective of the Apple device they are using. FaceTime is an exclusive Apple video chatting application that makes communication seamless for people who want to stay in touch. FaceTime video calling

quality is also one of the best in the industry and is highly encrypted, making it one of the premium features for your iPad.

Communication becomes more immersive and expressive with the latest spatial audio technology introduced in iPad Os 15.

The newest iPad versions also provide SharePlay to make it easy for people to watch movies or listen to music together while in a FaceTime call.

To get the most out of the FaceTime in your iPad, head over to Settings>FaceTime and turn on the FaceTime feature.

When you turn on the FaceTime feature on your iPad, it will use your Apple ID to connect to the FaceTime application. Click on the "Use Apple ID" option present in the same interface to enter your Apple ID password.
If you use a cellular iPad, your mobile number can also be used to reach you on FaceTime

How to Make FaceTime Calls

You need another person's Apple ID or mobile number to make a FaceTime call.

● Head over to the FaceTime application and click on "New FaceTime" to add a number or email address.

● Once done, click on the FaceTime icon or Audio button to start a video or voice call.

● You can also add multiple numbers to make a Group FaceTime.

● While in a FaceTime call, you can use SharePlay to watch movies or listen to music together. You can also use animated emojis while talking with your friends and family.

iMessage

iMessage is one of the few messaging apps restricted to only a particular system.

While traditional messaging apps like WhatsApp and telegram rule the Android space, Apple users are already equipped with a well-functioning messaging platform in the form of iMessage. You can use both Wi-Fi and cellular service to use it from your device.

iMessage is the default messaging app for your device. As iMessage is exclusively available for Apple devices, if the other party in the transaction doesn't have an Apple device, your message will be sent to them as a Short Message Service (SMS) or Multimedia Message Service (MMS) message.

All your messages are highly encrypted, and hence iMessage boasts its security system.

How to Sign In to iMessage

To sign in to iMessage, make sure that you are logged in with your Apple ID, or that your mobile number is active if it is a cellular iPad.

Go to Settings>Messages and turn on the "iMessage" option.

If you log in with the same Apple ID on different devices, all of your messages will automatically be synced and reflected on those devices.

How to Send and Receive Messages

With the Messages app, you can send text messages, photos, videos, Memojis, and audio messages.

iMessage is a fun application, and provides opportunities to send messages with animated effects, iMessage apps, and many other premium options for Apple iPad users.

With iMessage, you can send a text message to one or more people at one time.

● Click on the icon with a pen on the top of the screen to create a new message. If there is an existing conversation, you can click on it to send a message.

● In the "To" section, enter the numbers or contact names to whom you are trying to send a message.

• After choosing the contacts, head over to the text field and enter your text message. After completing the message, click on the arrow button with a blue arrow mark to send your message to the recipient.

• In the same way, you can respond to messages by tapping on a particular conversation and entering the text field. You can also use emojis whenever you want from the keyboard.

While in the Messages app you can press on the FaceTime icon to create a video call with the contact at any time.

How to Send Attachments

The iMessage app makes it easy to send photos and videos with just a click. Just click on the camera icon to take a new photo, or choose one or many images from the iPad. Once added, click on the blue arrow button to send these attachments.

In iPad Pro and Air models, you can use the inbuilt Camera app to send photos with filters and Memojis. You should have at least iPad OS13 for these additional features to appear on your Messages app.

How to Send Audio Messages

Audio messages can be a great way to convey a long text with just a few

seconds of speech. In the iMessage app, if you want to send a voice message to contacts, hold the icon that looks like waves before your "Send" button. It will record the message. You can click "x" anytime during this recording to stop sending the message. Once the recording is completed, click on the blue arrow button to send it.

By going to Settings>Messages, you can select the time at which these audio messages can expire.

How to Animate Messages

The iMessage app provides breathtaking animated effects for all of your messages. You can also send handwritten messages with the help of the digital feature provided. Turn your iPad to landscape mode and swipe the menu above the keyboard to use these animated messages or full-screen effects. Tap on the respective unique animated feature you want to try and click the blue arrow to send it to the recipient.

iMessage Apps

Apple also provides access for third-party application developers to create exclusive content such as sticker packs and easy link sharing via iMessage apps. For example, if you have Spotify installed on your iPad, you will unlock the feature to share any Spotify songs directly to your contacts via iMessage. Like the animated effects feature, you need to first swipe above the onscreen keyboard and select one of the iMessage apps to explore its features.

Memojis

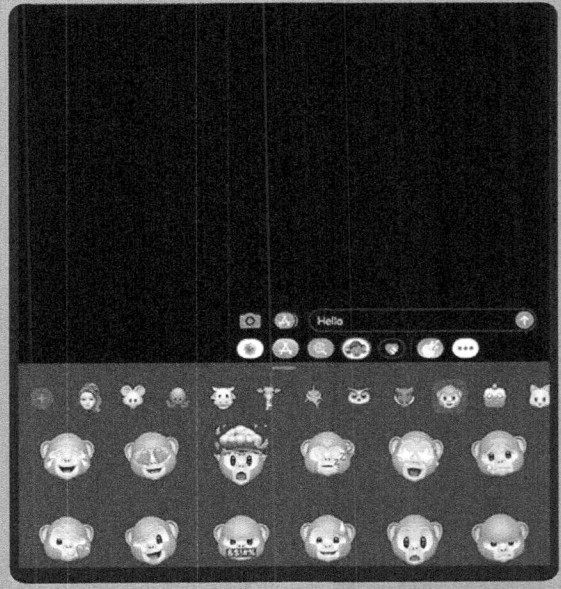

Memojis are an advanced version of emojis.

They are interactive and can help you bond or have fun with your closest people.

You can create personalized Memojis to send to your family and friends.

If using iPad Pro models, you can animate emoji stickers by recording your voice and using a real-depth camera to mirror your facial expressions.

Send or Receive Money

If you have Apple Pay installed and you have saved your cards to it, then you can easily send money from the iMessage app itself by clicking on the Apple Pay button in the iMessage app.

Once in the iMessage app, you can select the amount you would like to send, along with your authentication details.

Once verified, your money is immediately sent to the recipient's bank account.

Mail

Electronic mail - email - is one of the preferred ways to communicate with people worldwide. Businesses all around the world use email as a preferable way to connect their employees and contact their customers.

Apple provided an inbuilt Mail application for iPad users to easily send, receive, or read new email. You can link any email accounts such as GMail, Yahoo Mail, or Rediff mail to this application.

Go to Settings>Mail and click on the "Add Account" button to add the email account of your favorite service.

How to Check Your Mail

Click on the Mail app and head over to "Inbox," present on the top left of the app. You will be able to read all of the new mail that you have received. Unread emails will usually have a small blue dot beside them. When you read them, these dots will disappear.

How to Send Email

To send a new email, click on the last icon that looks like a note on the top right of the Mail app.

A new pop-up will arise where you can enter the recipient's email address, your message, and any attachments you may want to add.
Once written, click on the blue arrow button to send the email.

To add attachments, just click on the photo icon and add any images or videos to your message.

WhatsApp

WhatsApp is a popular messaging app for iPads.
WhatsApp is owned by Facebook and can help you easily communicate with your friends who use an Android phone. While the native messages app is a great communication app for iPad users, it is however exclusive to Apple devices.

Go to the App Store and search "WhatsApp" on the search tab to download WhatsApp to your device. Once downloaded, you need to verify your mobile number with the one time password received.

You can click on the "+" button to start a new conversation with contacts from your device. WhatsApp provides stickers for more interactive communication. All your messages are end-to-end encrypted, making all the communications secure.

Note: Whatsapp's Team declares that the official app for iPad will be arriving in the future. At this moment, the official app is only for iPhone devices. You can install the iPhone app on your iPad. It is only necessary to search apps in the App Store, paying attention to search in the app section for iPad and iPhone and not only iPad's apps.

Creating Accounts in Social Media Networks

As said before, social media networking apps such as Instagram, Facebook, and TikTok are all accessible from your iPad.

To open an account with any app, go to the App Store and search for the app. Once you have found the app, click on the "Get" button to download it to your device.

Now, head over to the home screen and click on the app you have downloaded. All these applications will start with a start screen where you have to either log in to your account or sign up for one.

Click on the "Signup" button to create an account for the respective platform.

Enter your basic details such as name, mobile number, address, and age for creating a new account.

You may have to verify your identity via email or mail. Once verified, your account will be created, and you can now use the "Login" to enter into the app and explore the possibilities they provide.

CHAPTER 4:
iPad Camera

The camera is an essential hardware component for any device these days. The first iPad released in 2010 doesn't have a camera, but the second generation released in 2011 included both front and rear cameras. Since then, iPads have been equipped with two high-quality cameras for the users. While iPad camera lenses are not as high quality as the iPhones, they still possess great cameras. To take better photos and videos using the camera app, you need to be aware of various options.

Head over to the home screen and click on the camera app to start using your camera. Alternatively, you can also ask Siri to open the camera using the "Hey Siri! open the camera" command.

Understanding Photos App

iPad cameras are powerful and allow you to take photos in different photo formats such as JPEG, PNG, and TIFF.
iPads inbuilt camera supports square or panorama mode. Higher-end models such as iPad pro also support portrait mode for better quality pictures.

With iPad, it is also easy to edit your pictures once taken and share them on different social media platforms or directly into your gallery. The photo-sharing feature and Apple's constant update process to iCloud also make it easy for individuals to make sure their photos are available across all their devices. **All your photos and videos taken by the camera will be present in the "Photos" app for you to look at.** These photos will also be categorized and divided into Albums for easier access. You can also create your custom albums for managing your Photo library efficiently.

How to Take Pictures With iPad Cameras?

• To make use of your camera, click on the "Camera" app on the screen

• In the bottom right of the screen, you will be able to select the mode for your camera such as video, photo, slo-mo, time-lapse, square, and pano. Depending on the iPad you are using, options may vary.

• Make sure that this option is on "Photo" for you to take high-quality photographs with your iPad. You can use autofocus or flash to enhance your pictures.

Once you have set the "Photo" option, click on the big circle on the screen to take a photograph. **The photo will be immediately saved to your "Photos" app.**

What Are the Other Options Available?

• Click on the small circle button above the camera button to shift between the rear and front-facing cameras.

● You can click on either the square or panorama options to take unique photos. The square option makes you take photographs that are in square shape and can be easily uploaded to image social networking apps such as Instagram. On the other hand, the pano option helps you to capture a panoramic display.

● You can click on the lightning bolt option to switch the flash option on or off. Flash helps you to take great photographs when there is less natural sunlight.

● You can use the "High Dynamic Range (HDR)" button to take underexposed and overexposed images.

● You can click on the timer icon to take photos with a short time limit.

● You can click on the top icon that looks like a bunch of circles to take live photos.

How to Take Videos With the iPad Camera?

iPads also provide powerful cameras to take cinematic and portrait videos.

Right now, only iPad Pro models provide cinematic quality for your videos. All the other iPads offer high definition (HD) quality videos for the users.

To start taking videos with your iPad, you should first select the video mode in your camera app. Just swipe down in the camera menu and you will enter the video mode.

When you are in video mode, the middle circle button becomes red.

It is a good sign to find out whether you are almost instantly in camera or video mode.

- You can now click on the red button for the video to start recording.

- On the top screen you will be able to see how much time it has been recorded.

- You can use a pinch gesture with your fingers to zoom in or out. You can also use volume up and down buttons to zoom in or out using your camera.

- When the recording is completed, you can click on the "stop" button for the video to stop.

Your video file will be automatically saved to your "Photos" app.

Other Video Modes

● You can click on the slo-mo mode to create videos that have fewer frames per second than the usual videos.

● You can click on the time-lapse mode to create videos for an extended period of time.

Use Live Text

Live text is a new iOS feature that works similar to Google Lens that works on Android devices. On all newer iPad models that can run iPad OS15, you can copy and share text that appears in between the camera frame.

How to Use Live Text?

● To use the live text feature, you need to use the camera app as usual.

● When the text is detected, it will show a yellow frame around it. You can now click on the icon that looks like a few lines between the camera to use it for live text features.

● Once the text is selected, you can either copy, translate, or share them by swiping the text.

Scan a QR Code

QR codes are right now a must for making transactions or verifying your authenticity without actually making physical contact.

Scanning QR codes is usually done by applications specifically. However, whenever you see a QR code, you can use your camera to detect the applications that it can take you to.

Open the camera and position your iPad so that the QR code gets detected. Once detected, a notification will appear to go to a website or an app.

Just click on it to redirect.

CHAPTER 5:
iPad Security

iPad is a device that focuses on providing privacy and security to the device user. All your data is encrypted and cannot be sniffed or accessed by anyone in the network. Apple also makes it very difficult for hackers to access your device by hardware manipulation. To get the maximum security advantage Apple provides for its users, you need to follow some or all of the below-mentioned practices.

Set a Strong Passcode

Passcode acts like a lock for your device.

It is the most common security feature Apple provides for all its device owners. Even if you have a Touch ID or Face ID installed, it is essential to have a passcode switched on for better encryption capabilities for all your content on the device.

• To set a strong passcode, head over to Settings and tap on "Passcode." Depending on the iPad model you are using, this option may be interlinked with either Touch ID or Face ID.

• Now turn on the passcode option and choose an alphanumeric to verify your device. It is usually recommended to use a four-digit numeric for remembering the lock code easily.

You should also know that for 10 failed passcodes, Apple provides you an option to delete your data or settings automatically for the perpetrator trying to get into your device that doesn't have any access to your files.

Touch ID

Touch ID is still the preferred authentication system for basic iPad and iPad Air models.

You need to register your fingerprint with the iPad to use Touch ID.

Head over to Settings > Touch ID & Passcode and follow the onscreen instructions.

Tap on "Add a Fingerprint" and place your finger on the screen for the device algorithms to recognize your fingerprint patterns. Once done, put your finger on the Home button (or near the top button if it is an Airpad model) to unlock your device or make purchases.

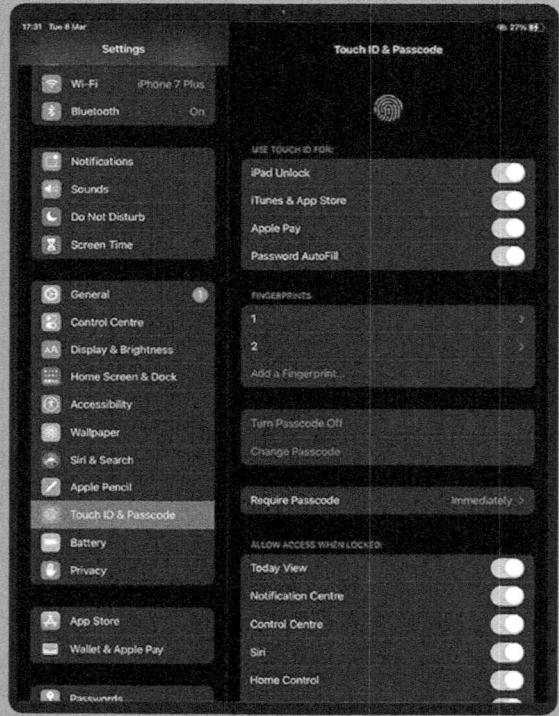

You can always add additional fingerprints from Settings > Touch ID & Passcode.

Face ID

FaceID is only available for newer iPad Pro models.
It can be used to unlock your phone, authorize purchases, or download apps onto your device.

However, remember that to use a FaceID, a passcode is mandatory. Because anytime Face ID doesn't work you may need to use your Passcode to unlock your device.

To set up Face ID, head over to Settings > Face ID & Passcode. When you click on the "Setup Face ID" button, a new interface will open up where you need to follow the onscreen instructions.

You may need to move your head according to the instructions provided for the motion sensors to detect your movements and understand your consistent patterns. Face ID uses complex machine algorithms to determine your face every time you try to unlock or make purchases with Face ID.

You can always add new Face IDs with different variations such as with a mask or with spectacles for your device by going to Settings > Face ID & Passcode.

What Can You Do With a Locked Screen?

While locked, even though you can't access applications on your device, you can perform some essential functions if you have been given access to the Settings menu.

- You can control what widgets to display on the locked screen

- You can look at the recent notifications

- You can give access to the control center

- You can give access to Siri

- You can return missed calls

- You can connect to a Mac or a Windows machine to control your Mac

- You can use a torch

- You can use camera

CHAPTER 6:
iPad Advanced Features

iPad has several advanced features that can help you get the most out of your device.

Screen Time

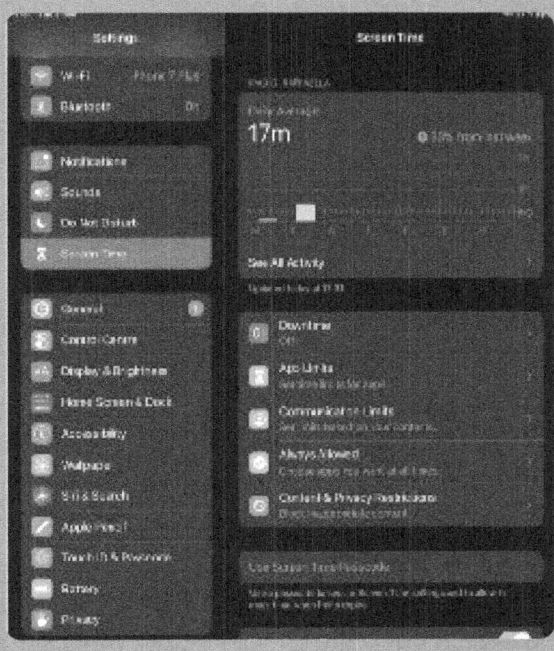

Screen Time is a premium feature provided by Apple for all iPad owners.

With Screen Time you can actively monitor how much time you spend on your device. You can also monitor how much time your family members spend on an iPad. Placing restrictions is also possible easily with the help of time limits that can be customized for different apps.

While Screen Time is a great feature, it still takes a significant part of your battery to track different apps and services.

And for this reason, Apple wants you to switch on this feature manually.

To activate the Screen Time feature, head over to Settings > Screen Time and tap on the "Continue" button.
Now you will get a pop-up to set up the screen time limit for your device.
You can also set screen time limits for your child on your child's iPad. Connecting the Screen Time feature with other Apple devices can share your Screen Time details across all your devices.

Any time, you can look at the report of your device with the information about how much time you have spent on different apps. Your report can be summarized either by a week or by day, according to your requirements.
To share your Screen Time details across all devices connected to your Apple ID, go to Settings > Screen Time and turn on the "Share across devices" option.

How to Activate Downtime?

With a great device like the iPad, you are expected to lose a lot of time in a day. **iPad OS provides an easy way to restrict your excessive device usage by using the downtime feature.** When the downtime feature is activated, you can only use predetermined apps or receive available notifications.

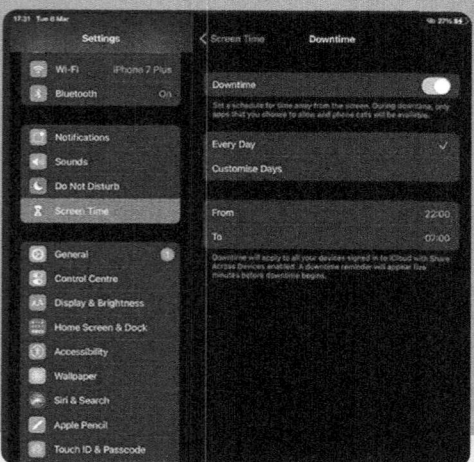

To activate this feature, head over to Settings > Screen Time and ensure that the Screen Time feature is turned on.
After confirmation, tap "Downtime" and turn it on to a specific schedule that works for you. You can also turn off the downtime option from the same menu. Downtime can also be done for a family member if family sharing is present.

How to Restrict Only a Particular App?

Not all apps consume a lot of your time. **iPad OS provides an easy way to limit a particular app or a category of apps using the Screen Time feature.**

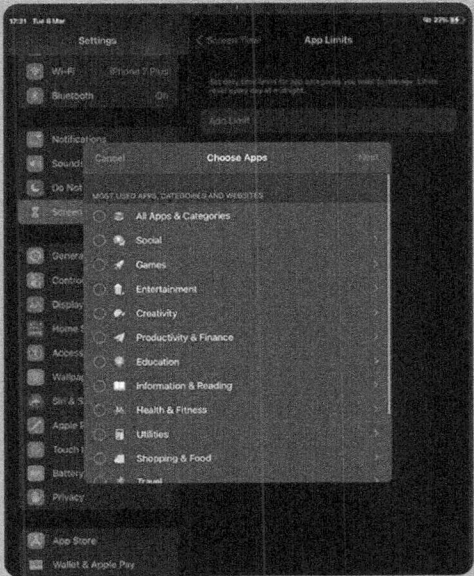

Go to Settings>Screen Time and click on "App Limits." Now you can select an individual app or a category of apps, and click "Next" to set the amount of time you wish to allow for an app or for a category of apps. Once your app limits are customized, tap on the "Add" button to finish setting up.

For example, if you are spending a lot of time scrolling Facebook instead of reading a book, you can restrict your usage of the Facebook app using the downtime feature. Once the allowed time is exceeded, the Facebook app can not be opened until the next day.

You can, however, temporarily turn off a time limit or delete a time limit from the same menu.

Set Communication Limits

iPad OS also provides an easy way to restrict communication with your contacts after a set amount of time. For this to work, make sure that your

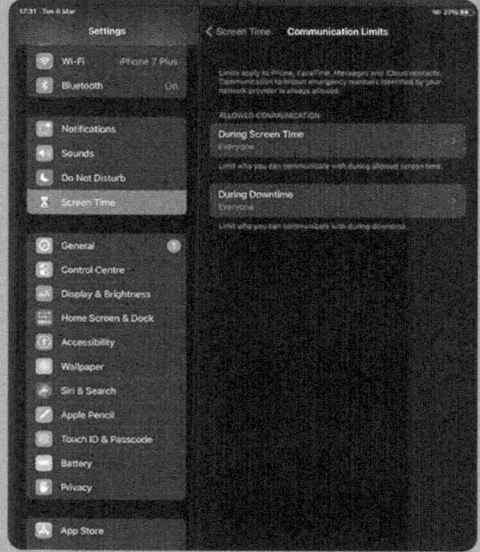

contacts are synced with iCloud.

To turn on and sync contacts with iCloud, head over to Settings > User name > iCloud and turn on the "Contacts" option in this menu.

Once the contacts are synced, head over to Settings>Screen Time and click on "Communication Limit."

Then you can choose one of the below options to set your communication limits.

• Contacts only
Your communication is restricted only to your contacts

• Everyone
Anyone can communicate with you

• Select contacts
You can select a few contacts from your contacts list

• Add new contact
New contact will be added to your contact list and will be allowed to communicate with you during downtime

Remember that all these limits can be easily temporarily removed or deleted by the user.

Hence, even though this feature acts as a reminder for you, your self-control is what makes you finally utilize these features.

Family Sharing

Apple makes it easy for family members to share subscriptions, manage devices, and share locations without actually sharing their account details. Family Sharing also makes it easy for parents to activate parental controls on their children's iPads.

To use Family Sharing, an adult family member should first create an organizer account and invite the remaining members to their family group. When family members join with the invite they can access shared content such as iCloud storage, Apple Music, Apple TV, Apple News, Apple Fitness, and Arcade.

To activate, head over to Settings > Your Device Name > Family Sharing and follow the onscreen instructions to set up an organizer account and share those links to your family members via iMessage or any other messaging app.

If you are trying to join a family group, click on the invitation you have received and click on the "'Join" button on the pop-up.

AirDrop

Apple Ecosystem provides an easy way to transfer files, photos, and links between iDevices such as iPhone, iPad, and Macs with the help of AirDrop technology.

AirDrop utilizes Bluetooth and Wi-Fi technology to send any file to other Apple devices quickly. It is much faster than Bluetooth or other file-sharing applications that use portable hotspot technology to transfer files.

What to Make Sure of Before Sending or Receiving Files

- Make sure that both Bluetooth and Wi-Fi are turned on.

- Make sure that the portable hotspot is turned off for both devices.

- Make sure that the files you receive are safe.

- To not get any files from devices which don't belong to someone from your contacts, just set the option to "receive from contacts only."

- If they are not in your contacts then you may need to select "everyone" for the file transfer to happen without any problems.

How to Use AirDrop

Open any file such as an image, video, or app link that you want to send, and click on the "Share'" button present.

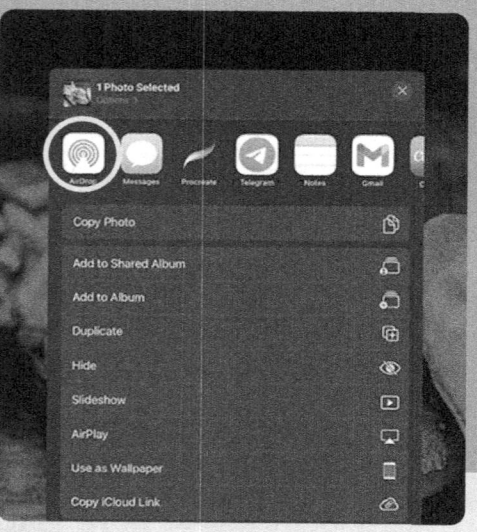

In the options you can see the AirDrop button. Click on it for a new pop-up to arise on your device. In this interface, you are able to see the names of the devices and people that are around you. Please select one of the people or devices to send your file(s) to them.

The person you have sent a request will get a pop-up on their screen. If they accept your submission, your AirDrop transfer will start.

AplePay

AplePay is the official payments app for all Apple devices. It is more secure than the other payment apps available, and is highly encrypted, making your card details safe. With AplePay, it becomes easy to send or receive money from family and businesses right from the messages app.

To add your credit or debit card details to Apple Pay, Go to Settings>Wallet & Apple Pay and tap on the "Add Cards" option. Remember that adding cards will not be possible without logging into Apple ID, as it acts as an essential factor for encryption.

Whenever you tap a saved card, you will have an option to change the card's details. You can change the billing address and look at the card's activity from your device. There is also an option to remove the card from your wallet by pressing the "Delete" option.

What are AppClips?

App Clips are small parts of apps that can automatically help you make payments by scanning QR and App Clip codes.

To use an app, check the code using the camera, and after verification the amount will be automatically debited from your stored Apple Pay card.

You can go to Settings > App Clips to look at the clips available from your installed apps. You can click "Delete" on any of the clips to not use them anymore.

Clock

Apple's Clock app provides an easy way to set up an alarm or look at the time for different cities effortlessly from your iPad. It can also perform other simple tasks such as acting as a stopwatch and a timer for the iPad user. When you tap on the Clock app present on the home screen, you will be taken into an interface that displays the world clock. There will be different cities listed on the world map by default. You can manage these cities by adding or editing using the "+" button present on the top right of the screen.

You will be immediately able to choose a city from the list.

• When you tap on the city, it will be immediately added to your world clock.

• To delete a city from the world clock, click on the "Edit" button present on the top left of the screen. Now head over to the city you want to delete and tap on "-" present on the city column. You can also reorder the cities by holding on to the column and moving it around to other columns.

• Once the actions are completed, click on "Done" to reflect the changes.

Now, in the same Clock app, click on the "Alarm" tab at the bottom of the screen. You will be taken into another interface where you can set the alarm for a specific time. While there are different third-party alarm apps in the App Store, all of them work only when the mobile screen is on; hence, for iPad users, the official Clock app provided by Apple is a better choice for setting the alarm.

• Click on the "+" button that is present on the top right of the screen to open a pop-up to set an alarm.

• In the first option, select the time you need to ring the alarm. Make sure that the time is set to AM or PM correctly.

Once the time is set you can use additional options to optimize your alarm.

● **Repeat**

This option will help you choose whether to use the alarm details for the next day.

● **Label**

This option helps you create a name for your alarm.

● **Sound**

This option helps you choose a tone for your alarm. Only the default ones provided by Apple can be used. Alternatively, you can select a downloaded Apple music song as your alarm tone by tapping on the "Pick a song" option.

● **Snooze**

This option makes your alarm ring after exactly nine minutes if you didn't turn it off.

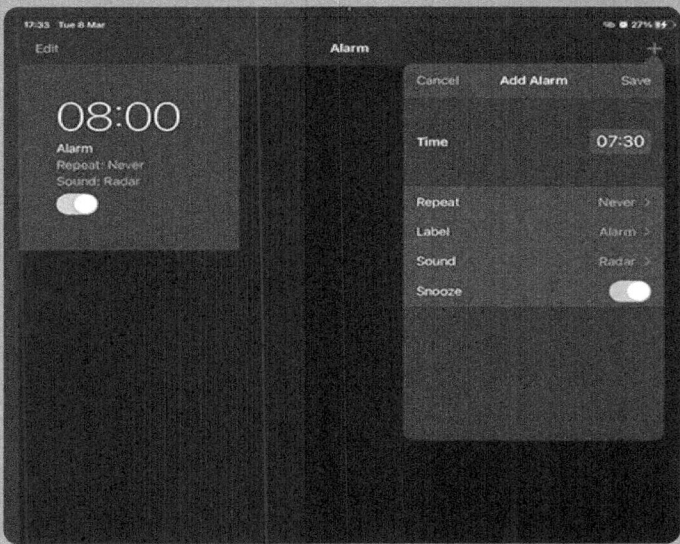

Once the options are given, click on the "Save" button to save the alarm.

You can always click on the "Edit" button to change or delete alarm details anytime.

Calendar

iPad users can use a calendar app to create events for different appointments and meetings.

The calendar app's primary focus is to ensure that your work and personal schedules are as organized as possible. Your friends and family from your contacts can also invite you easily via the Messages app to join any events.

There are different ways to add events to your calendar. The most convenient is to use Siri to add or edit any events.

- "Hey Siri, set up a meeting at lake view for tomorrow at 10 AM"
- "Hey Siri, do I have a meeting today?"
- "Hey Siri, postpone all events from today to tomorrow."

If you are not comfortable with Siri, you can use the Calendar app to add or edit events.

How to Add an Event

First of all, open the app and tap on the date you want to schedule an event. Click on the "+" icon once you are on day view. Click on the I+" icon to

create a new event.

In the new interface, enter the title and location of the event. You can also add a link to the video call if it is a remote event.

In the same way, enter other details such as start and end time, or travel time necessary for the event. You can also add small snippets in the notes section for any remarks about the event.

Once all the required information is entered, click on the "Add" button to schedule an event.

How to Add an Alert to the Event

To add an alert, select the "Alert" option on the pop-up and choose when you need to get an alert for your event.
In the Settings>Sounds option, you can also change the tones for the event alerts. There are only a few default options available for tone alerts. You can also add attachments such as images and .pdfs by clicking on the "Add Attachment" button.

iTunes Store

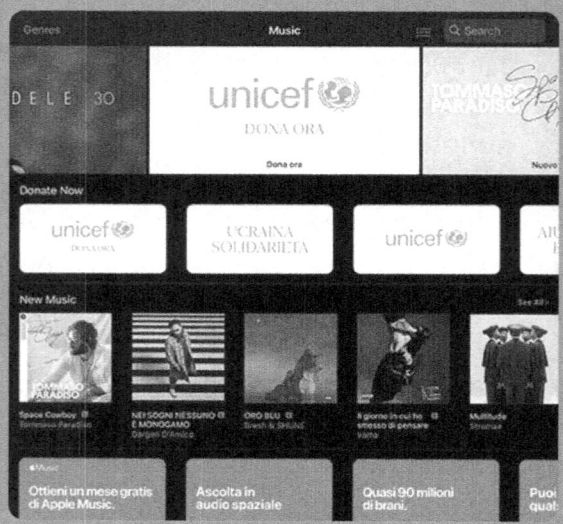

iTunes Store is Apple's official store for buying music, images, and videos.

To access iTunes Store you need to have an Apple ID, and should enter eligible payment details. Moreover, different iTunes stores have various content restrictions.

Tap on the "iTunes Store" app present on the home screen to purchase and add your favorite music, movies, and TV shows to your library.

How to Find Content

When on the app interface, you will choose your favorite category by selecting the tabs present on the bottom of the screen: Music, Movies, and TV Shows.

There are also three special sections for users to quickly find content on the platform.

• Top Chart displays all the popular content according to your region.
• Genius displays recommendations based on your history and past purchases.
• Using the search tab, you can search a vast library of songs, movies, and ringtones.

iTunes Store also provides a preview for all the songs present in the library.

To buy an item from the iTunes Store, click on the price present beside the item. You will be automatically asked to enter your Apple ID password to confirm your transaction.

How to Get Ringtones

Apple provides many default ring and notification tones, but customization is difficult. Unlike Android phones, it is not easy to directly transfer MP3 files to a mobile device to set it as a ringtone.

Instead, you need to purchase a ringtone from the iTunes Store and activate it accordingly. There are thousands of tones available as a ringtone on the iTunes Store. Choose a category of your wish to have different tones available. Once downloaded, all your tones will automatically be added to the Settings menu to help you easily choose a ring or notification tone.

Shortcuts App

The Shortcuts app provided by Apple to its users is one of the best personalization and automation applications available for iPad users. With the Shortcuts app, you can download YouTube videos, automatically switch on or off your smart home equipment, and turn your device into energy-

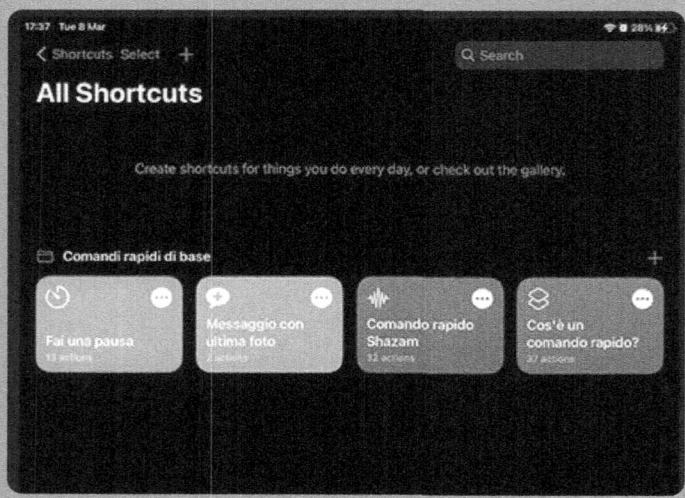

saving mode automatically, without your interference.

Many predefined options can give you control of all the native apps provided.

With a little bit of effort, you can continually expand the horizons of the capabilities that the Shortcuts apps can achieve.

How to Create an Easy Shortcut

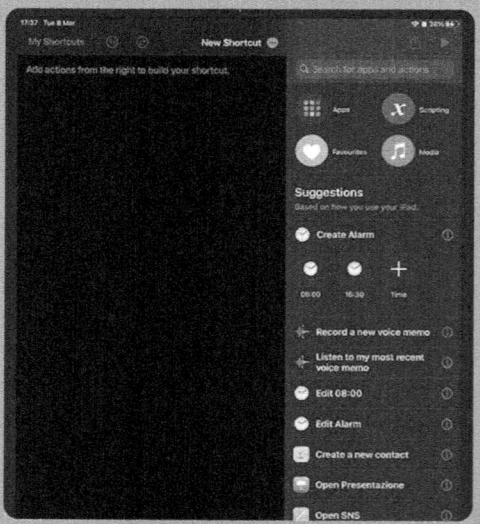

● Go to the Shortcuts app and click on the "+" button on the upper right corner.

● A new pop-up will come up where you need to enter your shortcut's name.

● Once the shortcut is created, you can click on the "Add Action" button to start adding blocks to your shortcut.
There are several default actions you can choose from if you want to create a simple shortcut. On the other hand, creating a

custom action increases complexity but provides a lot of opportunities for the user to achieve.

● Add multiple actions to create a workflow.

● Once all the actions are added, click on the play button to test the shortcut. You can click on the stop button to end the shortcut while testing it.

Some Custom Shortcuts

● Automatically opening a quick note when your alarm snoozes.

● Automatically turning off your mobile data if your mobile data is low.

● Automatically switching on Airplane mode.

Stocks App

In this modern economic world investment is necessary for every individual.
Many iPad users already have a portfolio that they must constantly follow to be aware of market movements that affect their investments. Apple provides a default "Stocks" app for iPad users to easily track their stock performance.

1. Add stocks to your watchlist

As there are a lot of stocks available, it is suggested that the user add their favorite stocks to their watchlist.

Just search for your favorite stock using the company name, ticker symbol, or fund name and click on "Add" to get it into your watchlist.

Once added, you can remove them anytime from the list using the "-" button. You can also rearrange them by holding and moving them with your fingers.

2. Look at charts

The Stock app provides a lot of information for the user.

You can look at charts that describe how the stock has performed over a specific period. You can also look at other stock-specific information such as P/E, dividend value, market value, and daily price change.

3. Read news

From iPad OS14 onwards, the Stocks app is filled with news articles for different stocks. If you are subscribed to the Apple News feature, you may also be able to read more articles specific to your favorite stock.

Maps App

The Maps app helps iPad users to quickly look at maps provided by Google.

Switching on your GPS using location services can help map applications detect your location with GPS help.

In the Maps app, you can quickly zoom in or out of the maps using the pinch technique.

How to Search for a Location on Maps

You can use the Maps app to search addresses, cities, and locations across the planet.

You can use the search tab on the top of the screen to search any location. Once you get the results, click on the relevant one to display it on Maps.

You can also use Siri to find nearby restaurants or tourist attractions.

The Apple Maps application also provides easy access to popular destinations nearby your location.

Tip: You can click on any location, such as a restaurant displayed on the map, to get information and public reviews about it.

All this data is usually pulled from Google Maps, and hence it can be considered reliable.

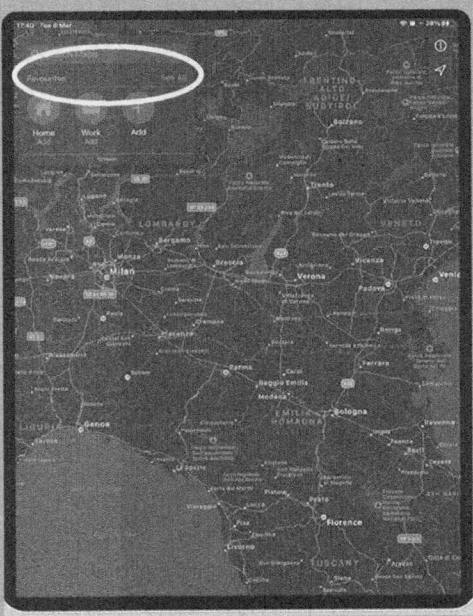

CHAPTER 7:
Troubleshooting Issues With Your iPad

There are different ways to turn off or restart your iPad using the Settings option. Sometimes you may encounter freezing issues, or if your iPad gets stuck because of an application or due to excessive usage.

What to Do

• For newer iPad Pro models, you can press the top button and either of the volume buttons for three seconds simultaneously so that the iPad can reboot.
• For older iPad models, you can press and hold just the top button for more than three seconds so that the iPad can reboot.

You can confirm the reboot of an iPad when the Apple logo appears on your screen.

Alternatively, for any iPad model, you can go to Settings>General and click on the "Shutdown" button for the slider to appear on the top of the screen. The iPad will shut down when you drag the slider to the other end.

If your iPad is frozen or doesn't respond for whatever reason, you can perform the below basic troubleshooting steps.

• Press and hold the top button for more than 10 seconds
• Press and quickly release the volume button nearer to the top button
• Press and quickly release the volume button further to the top button
• Press and hold both top and home buttons for more than 10 seconds

If your iPad still doesn't respond, then either contact Apple Support or visit the nearest Apple Store for a technician to check the problem with the device.

How to Update iPad OS

Every few months Apple provides updates to all its devices. Even though you update your devices, your settings and applications will remain the same. Updates offer more stability and add new features for your device.

For example, in iPad OS15, you can add widgets to your home screen, whereas iOS14 doesn't have that feature. We suggest you regularly check the updates because many security bugs will be patched during the updates, making your iPad more secure.

There is an option to update the iPad OS either automatically or manually.

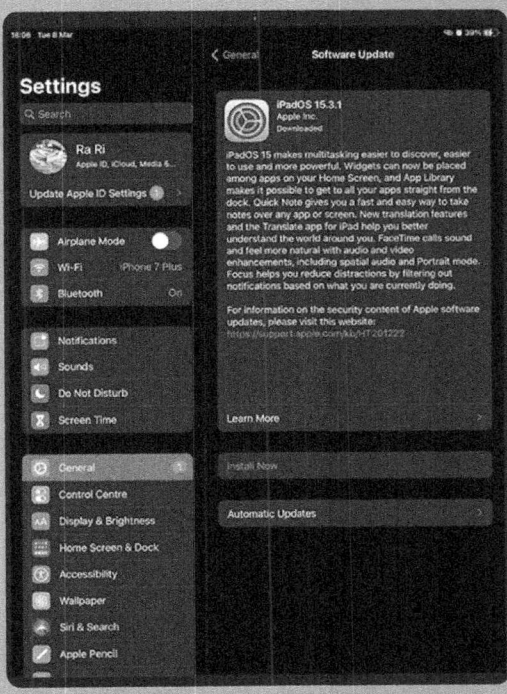

To automatically install device updates go to Settings>General>Software Update, and turn on the "Automatic Updates" option. Whenever there is a system update, the file will be automatically downloaded and updated overnight when connected to a power source.

If, for any reason, you want to update your system manually, then first go to Settings>General>Software Update and turn off the "Automatic Updates" option.

Now, whenever you want to update your system, go to Settings>General>Software Update for the newer software version to appear.

When you are ready, click on the "Download and Update" button for the iPad to be updated to the latest version of iPad OS.

You can also update your iPad OS when connected to your computer or Mac using a USB cable.

In the iTunes application or Mac finder sidebar, click on the "Check updates" button for the software to find any new updates for your device.
If there are any updates available, the file will be downloaded, and your iPad will be updated automatically. However, you mustn't remove the USB from your device while this process continues.

How to Backup Your iPad

Backing up your device helps you restore your data if there is any problem with your device during the update, or when you restore your device to the default setting.

You can also use this backup to easily export all your data to a new iPad.

Most of the time, users will be backing up their data with the help of iCloud Backup.

To turn on iCloud Backup, go to Settings>Device Name>iCloud and turn on the "iCloud Backup" option. You can also select whether or not to use cellular data for backup in these settings. When the option is turned on, iCloud will automatically backup your device settings when connected to Wi-Fi and locked. You can also use a Mac finder or Windows Itunes to perform a backup.

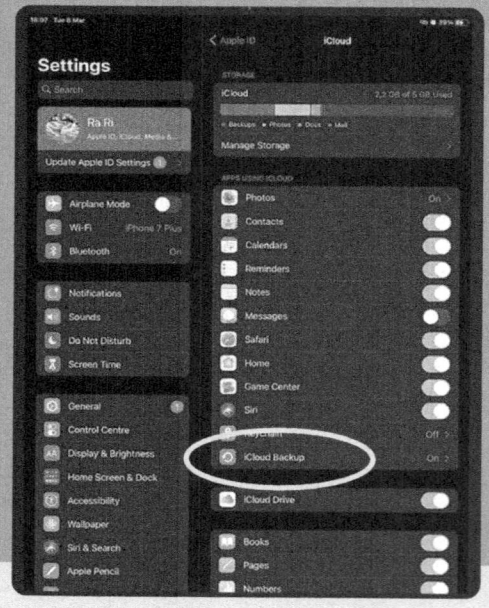

How to Restore From a Backup

To restore from a backup, you need to be connected to Wi-Fi and should be able to access your iCloud Backup files using your Apple ID.
After selecting the language and region during the device installation setup, select the option "Set Up Manually" to choose an iCloud Backup. Once selected, your iPad will be installed with your previous settings.

How to Return iPad Settings to Default

Sometimes iPad users may want to reset their iPad to factory default settings, or erase their iPad to start fresh. It is pretty easy to perform these tasks from the Settings menu.

● To reset all system settings for your iPad, go to Settings>General>Transfer or Reset iPad>Reset, and click on the "Reset All Settings: option.
This will remove system settings such as privacy, home screen, sound, display, and screen time, personalization, and location from your device, and will restore to the default options.

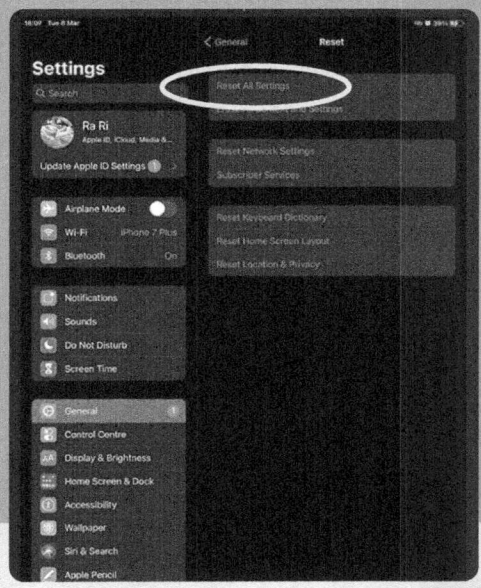

● You can also use "Reset All Networking options" in the same menu to erase the custom network settings and replace them with the default networking settings. All your VPN access points will also be removed when clicking on this option.

If you want to remove only VPN configuration profiles, go to Settings>General>Profiles & Device Management, and click on your VPN profile. Once the VPN profile is highlighted, you will see it with a red color font. Click and confirm it to remove this profile.

How to Erase an iPad

Remember that the "Erase iPad" option will remove all your data from the device. So, perform these steps with caution.

These steps are usually performed when you sell your device or give it away to someone. It is recommended that users perform a backup before executing this operation.

Go to Settings>General>Transfer or Reset iPad, and click on the Erase All content and Settings" option to start the operation.

The device will display a pop-up to confirm that you will be ok with the content erase.

When you click "Yes," your iPad will be erased, and an Apple logo will appear, indicating that the device is being restarted for a fresh install.

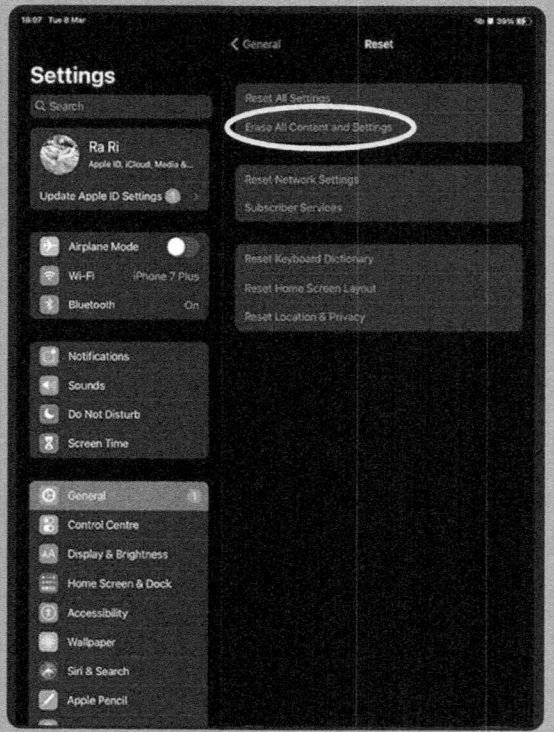

CHAPTER 8:
Reading On an iPad

Books have been the primary source of knowledge for humans for thousands of years. Even with the advancement of different mediums for people to understand, books are still the most intriguing way to recharge your conscious mind. **The iPad can act as a splendid reading device compared to laptops and desktops because you can place the iPad just like a book on your palm.** Even though iPads are not total e-readers like Kindle and Nook e-readers, they are still the best electronic device to read books, newspapers, magazines, and comics, with the ability to make annotations and notes as seamlessly as possible. You can also use accessories such as an Apple Pencil to edit documents and books, just like how you can on a paperback book.

How to Buy Books

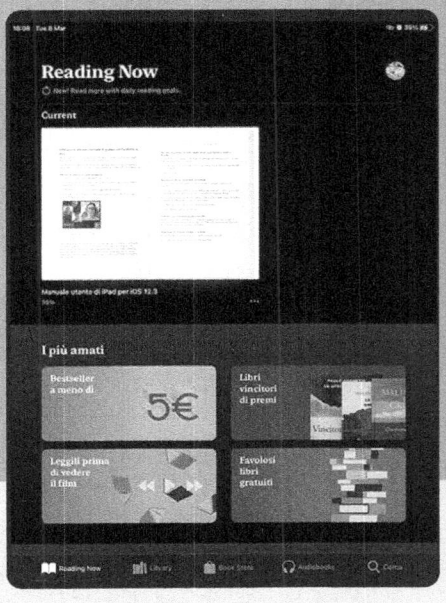

Apple uses its default book reading application called "Books" to let iPad users read books of different formats. You can download books directly from the Apple Books Store or import from other sources to your "Books" application. Apple BookStore offers millions of free and paid books for Apple users.

To buy new books, tap on the Books app on the home screen to be taken to the app.

You can now click on the "Book Store" tab to buy any free or paid book. You can search from millions of books and audiobooks available for iPhone and iPad users. Click on the "Get" button present beside books to download these books to your library if they are free. If they are paid books, you need to enter your payment information for them to download to your library.

All purchases need an active Apple ID for them to go through. Before buying, make sure that you have looked at the Apple Store preview for users to test whether the book is of desirable quality that works for them.

How to Read Books

Once you have downloaded the book(s), they will be sent to the "Library" tab of the app. Just click on the book cover to open the book in Apple's inbuilt Ebook reader. Remember that by default Apple Books application supports only .epub and .pdf files. If you want to read any document formats other than these, such as .mobi, it is impossible.

Reading Now

This section will display all the books that you are currently reading. It will show progress for each book that you are reading. You can also manage your reading goals and easily track your reading progress from this section.

Library

This section provides all the books and audiobooks that you have either imported or downloaded from the Book Store.

You can click on the "Collections" options present on the top of the screen to look at different collections that your books have been divided into.

You can also click on the "New Connection" button to create a customized collection of books.

Once you click on a book, you will access the default reader. It has advanced document reading futures, and with time Apple promises to increase the features for Ebook readers.

• You can turn the pages by swiping from left to right or from right to left. You can also tap any part of the screen to turn to the next or previous page quickly.

• You can adjust the screen brightness by dragging the slider.

• You can adjust the font of the book if it is of .ePub format using the "Aa" button.

• You can also change the background color for better reading during the night.

• You can enable the vertical scrolling option using the toggle button.

• You can bookmark any page in the book by clicking on the bookmark icon present on the top left of the screen.

• You can select any word or any sentence in the book to create a quick note for it.

Notes App

The Notes app helps iPad users create quick notes, checklists, or write a whole manuscript if you want to. Even though it isn't a robust word processor such as Microsoft Word or Google Docs, it still works efficiently for daily usage.

How to Create a Blank Note

Click on the Notes app on the home screen to open the application.
Once in the Notes app, click on the last icon on the top left that looks like a pen on the paper to create a new blank note.

Once the note is created, the first sentence you will add will be the title of the note, which will appear in the Notes library.

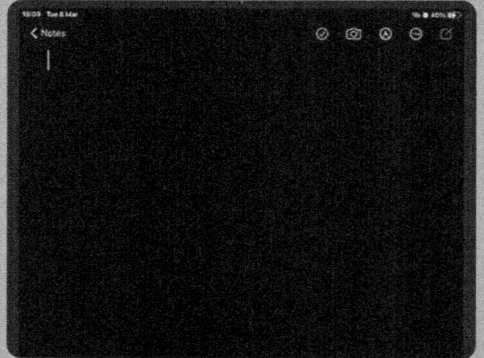

How to Format

For any text in the Notes app, you can click on the "Aa" icon just above the keyboard to format the text. You need to select the text you want to format to work as intended.

Once the note is written and formatted, you can click on the "Save" button for the note to be saved.

Advanced Options

Notes app provides advanced features for iPad users to perform various tasks with just a few clicks.

1. Checklists

Checklists are a great way to organize your tasks.

For example, while shopping, you can use these checklists to confirm whether or not you have shopped for particular items.

After tapping on the item, you will add new items to the list. Just click on the enter button to head over to the next item in the list.

You can format all the list items using the "Aa" button.
You can tap on the circle beside the checklist to mark it as completed.
You can also sort all the completed list items for better viewing.
You can click on the circle or marked checklist to reorder the items in the list.

2. Editing a Table

Tables can be a great way to enter analytical and statistical information into a note.

Click on the icon beside the "Aa" button that looks at a table to create a default "2x2" table. You can further add rows and columns by clicking on the icons present on the table to select whether to create a new row or column.

3. Drawing and Writing in the Notes App

Click on the icon that looks like a pen on the top of the screen.
You will enter into scribble mode to draw or write on the notes app using Apple Pencil.

This section has different markup tools to change your writing color, size, and pattern.
You can also use the eraser option to undo any drawings quickly.
If present in split-screen mode, you can drag any pictures or other written text using an Apple Pencil.

4. Adding Attachments

For better note-taking ability, it is essential to have a way to quickly add different attachments such as photos, videos, or scanned document texts.

Apple also makes it easy to add maps or links to other documents and web links right from here.

Click on the "Camera" icon present to add attachments.
You can select any photo from the gallery or can use live photos.

Translate

Apple made it easy for iOS users to translate their text from one language to another using the default "Translate" app.

The Translate app is available exclusively from iOS15 on. If you are using an iPad OS version below 15, you will not be able to translate your text easily. You can, however, install other third-party translators such as Google Translate from the app store to satisfy your translating needs.

Note: Only less than 20 languages are available to translate. With time, however, additional languages will be added.

Tap on the Translate app to open the application.

You can select the languages you want the translation for on the initial screen.

For example, English and Mandarin can be selected to convert your English text to Mandarin script. If you want to convert a Mandarin script to English text, you should choose Mandarin as the source language and English as the destination language.

You can also tap on the microphone symbol present on the bottom of the screen to say a phrase and translate it into another language.

When the translated text appears on the screen, you can utilize four options provided by the app.

1. You can play the audio translation by tapping on the play icon

2. You can save the translation by tapping on the star icon

3. You can look up different words in the translation by tapping on the book icon

4. You can enlarge the translated text by tapping on the enlarge icon

The Translate app also provides a conversation mode for iPad users, apart from the translation model. This feature can be helpful when two people with different native languages need to converse in real time.

All you have to do is open the app in conversation mode and tap on the screen for the device to detect your voice and translate it into another language to respond to the app, and it can translate back to you. The iPad will automatically detect your voice from the following conversation without tapping the screen.

Offline Translation

iPad also can translate without any internet connection by downloading the language packs onto your device.
To download your required languages, go to Settings>Translate and tap "Downloaded languages." In the following interface, select the down arrow icon beside your required language to download it to your device.

After downloading, click "Turn on-Device Mode", and whenever there is no internet, the phrases and words will be translated using these language packs.

Advanced Translate Features

iOS15 also makes it easy to translate in-app text or images using some of the new and improved features.

1. Select the text you want to translate in any app and hold it to get a few options to pop up. Now, select the Translate button to replace the text with another language text.

2. On newer iPad Pro models, you can scan an image and select the icon with three lines nearer the photo options to detect text and automatically translate it into your favorable language. This is quite similar to how Google Lens works on Android devices.

News

News is the brand new iPad application that helps iPad users easily explore news from different popular websites from their region from one interface. You can personalize the news articles that will be displayed on the application. At present, the News application is available only in a few regions.

How to Get Personalized Content

To get personalized news articles on your News application, you need to add different channels for your account.
You can also search for various topics and add them by clicking on the "+" button.

Apple also provides a new subscription service called Apple News+ to read from hundreds of local and international magazines.

How to Read Stories

Whenever you find a story that you like from the recommendations provided, click on the articles to open in the Apple News inbuilt reader.

You can also quickly swipe left or right to go to the next or previous article.

• By clicking on the "aA" button you will be able to change the font size settings.

• You can easily share the settings by clicking on the icon with three dots.

• You can also quickly look at the details of the magazine in which the story was published and look at different issues that are available for you to read.

You can also download these issues to your offline storage to read them without the internet.
If the offline issues are no longer needed, you can click on the bin icon to delete them permanently.

CHAPTER 9:
Siri and Apple Music

Siri is one of the favorite features for many users who love the Apple Ecosystem. Siri is an intelligent voice assistant that can understand your voice commands and provide answers in return. Siri uses complex machine learning and artificial intelligence algorithms to ensure that the conversation is as natural as possible. Once you use different default Siri commands, Siri uses your behavior to craft responses. Every year Apple provides essential updates for Siri to make it better than all the other voice assistants such as Google Assistant and Alexa.

How to Activate Siri

Whenever you turn on the iPad for the first time, in the installation wizard, you will have the choice to activate Siri.

All you have to do is follow the on-display instructions and activate Siri.

We have already discussed starting Siri from the installation wizard in the first chapter.

Note: Remember that as Siri uses an internet connection to curate voice commands and

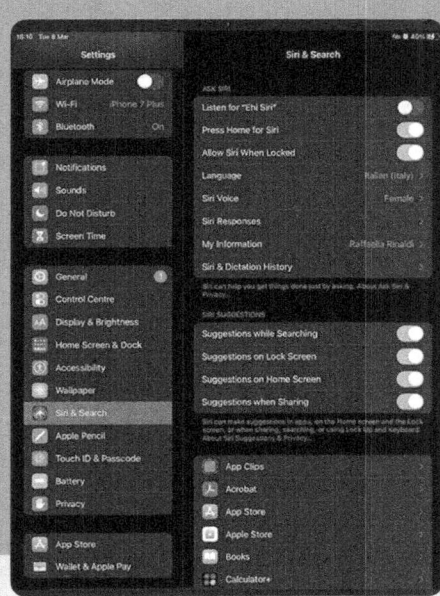

provide valid responses, you need to be connected to Wi-Fi or a mobile data connection to get the most out of Siri.

If you didn't install Siri using the installation wizard, you can always install it from Settings.

1. Tap the "Settings" icon on the home screen and click on the "Siri & Search" option present on the left side menu.

2. In the "Siri & Search" dialog, toggle the button beside the "Listen for 'Hey Siri;" option.

3. When you click on the toggle button, you will get a pop-up message that asks you to click on "Enable Siri."

4. Once you click on it, you will be asked to choose a voice for Siri.

You can either choose a male or female voice according to your preference. You can also change this after setting up Siri.

5. After choosing the voice, you will be asked by the interface to say "Hey, Siri" to recognize your voice and remember it for future instances.

For further recognition, you may need to speak five different variations of "Hey, Siri" commands shown on the screen.

6. Once the initial voice recognition is completed, Siri will be activated on your iPad, and from now on, whenever you say "Hey, Siri," your iPad will recognize your voice and provide you a response.

Other Settings

1. You can toggle on the "Home for Siri" button so that whenever you long-press the home button, Siri will be activated. If you are an iPad Pro user, this option will be replaced with "Press Top for Siri" to activate Siri.

2. You can choose the default language for Siri in the settings option. There are a lot of languages for you to choose from. By default, a language will be selected for you according to your location.

3. You can choose whether or not you want to use Siri while locked by toggling the "Allow Siri When Locked" option on/off.

4. Let Siri know the voice you want to use using the "Siri Voice" option. American, Australian, and British accents are some of the available varieties for the user.

5. You can also let Siri know more about you by selecting your information and selecting your contact.

What Else Can Siri Do?

There are thousands of different things that you can make Siri do for you. With time, these possibilities will only be exponentially increasing. Siri also allows various commands based on whether or not developers of the third-party app have included them during the development process.

For starters, you can hold the home button or top button for a few seconds for Siri to switch on. Still, if you don't say any commands during this time, Siri will automatically provide you with a few default options such as FaceTime, messages, App Store, and Translation on the screen.

This default menu is usually customized and depends on what you use.

As Siri uses artificial intelligence and deep learning to understand your commands, it is not mandatory to follow specific commands. Even if you twist words or use synonyms, Siri will analyze and understand what you are expecting from it. However, for better results, it is recommended to use a basic structure of commands.

Get Suggestions

To get some suggestions based on your recent activity on the device from Siri, head over to the home screen and swipe down using your finger.

You will get a search text field along with a "Siri Suggestions" column that lists some of the suggestions for you.

You can click on any of the options on the screen to take you to your last place in the app.

Additionally, sometimes Siri will also list news stories according to your recent articles.

Call Contacts Using FaceTime

First of all, to work correctly, you need to enter your contact information in the "My Information" field. Once done, ensure that the number you are trying to call is registered as a contact on your iPad. You can also add your relationship status, such as Mom, Dad, or Wife, using the related name field in the Contacts app.

1. Press the home button or invoke Siri using the command "Hey, Siri."

2. Once Siri is functioning, say the command "FaceTime Sam" or "Make a FaceTime call to bro." (You can replace "Sam" with a name in your contacts list, of course.)

3. Siri will immediately connect your call to the contact if there is only one match.

If, however, there are two or more possible matches, then Siri will ask you to select one either by screen or voice command.

4. Once the call is placed, you can end it anytime using the home button.

Create Reminders and Alerts

You can also use Siri to remind you about any event with alerts.
Hold the home or top button until you get the Siri notification and try saying one of the below commands.

- "Hey Siri, wake me up at 2.20 AM."

- "Hey Siri, alert me tomorrow about Sam's birthday."

- "Hey Siri, every Thursday, remind me about going to church."

You can always use Siri to cancel all the reminders or any specific reminder you have decided not to do today.

- "Hey Siri, cancel all events for today."

- "Hey Siri, delete all the alerts that you have for me today."

Adding Tasks to the Calendar

Siri can also be an excellent organizational tool by adding different tasks to your calendar.

Here are some examples of th commands you can say:

- "Hey Siri, set up a meeting at 3 PM tomorrow with my manager."

- "Hey Siri, set up a meeting in the afternoon tomorrow."

- "Hey Siri, set up dinner with my wife at 8 PM tomorrow."

Play Music

In 2022, Apple has started to provide a new Apple Music Voice service to help Apple users explore the vast Apple Music library using Siri.

Starting from just $4.99USD per month, you can interact with the music library using Siri commands.

However, remember that your audio doesn't support lossless or spatial audio using this version.

Here are some example commands:

- "Hey Siri, play Bob Dylan music."

- "Hey Siri play some chilling music,"

- "Hey Siri, play the ' This is my world ' playlist."

- "Hey Siri, play any song by The Beatles."

- "Hey Siri, play some fast beat songs for my workout."

- "Hey Siri, reduce the volume."

- "Hey Siri, play a random song."

- "Hey Siri, repeat the song until I stay 'stop.'"

Siri will constantly observe your listening patterns and try to suggest songs that you may like.

Apple Music

Music is eternal, and everyone tries to use their iPad at least once to listen to their favorite artist's music. The Apple iPad boasts a great sound system with Dolby support for the latest iPad versions. If you have a compatible Airpods version, you can also listen in a spatial audio format of high quality.

Apple comes with a default application called Music, which can listen to music files that you can listen to by sending them into your iPad using iTunes or by purchasing from the iTunes store. The music application also is the default user interface (UI) for Apple's music streaming service known as Apple Music. iPad users can also use Airdrop to easily share music files and open them in the Music application.

Apple Music is a subscription service offered by Apple for its customers. It boasts a collection of 75 million songs and provides both online and offline listening to subscribers. Apple Music costs $9.99USD per individual per month. You can get three months for free if you use Apple music on a new device. All you need is an Apple ID for activating your Apple Music subscription.

How to Activate Your Apple Music Subscription: Open the Music application on your dock and you will see a banner with "Subscribe" on it. Click on it to open a payment pop-up to activate your subscription. Use either Touch ID, Face ID, or your Apple ID password to start your subscription.

How to Listen to Music

Click on the Music app to access a new interface for all your listening needs. Selecting the "Show" tab presents different ways to organize or listen to your music.

You can use the "Search" tab to search songs from the Apple music library and your music library.

In the library section of the app, there are several options for you to choose from.

• You can click on the "Recently Played" section to listen to your recently listened to songs.

• You can click on "Albums" to look at different recommended albums according to your library.

• You can click on "Songs" to listen to individual tracks in your library.

• You can click on "Made For You" to look at the recommendations that Apple has made for you according to your listening patterns.

To listen to a track, click on the song to open using an inbuilt music player. The inbuilt musical player consists of:

• A play button
• A pause button
• A shuffle button
• A repeat button
• A lyrics button, which you can tap on to look at complete lyrics for the song
• Album art
• Add to Playlist button
• Download button for offline listening

- Streaming option for Airplay-enabled devices
- Skip to the next song
- Skip to the previous song
- More options button to look at album and artist details

In the newer versions of iOS, all Apple streaming services can use lossless technology to ensure high-quality content.

Apple Music Settings

You can change several settings in the settings menu for the Apple Music app.

●You can adjust equalizer settings for all the songs you play.

For example, classical or deep equalizer can have a lot of differences, especially while playing on high-quality headphones such as Airpods max.

- You can select whether or not to download an animated album cover.

- You can select whether or not to choose the automatic downloads option.

- You can select whether you want to play with mobile data or not if you have a supported cellular model.

- You can select whether or not to use lossless audio while downloading media

Podcasts on Your iPad

Apple also makes it easy to experience podcasts with a separate app.

Podcasts are an excellent medium for acquiring knowledge or exploring different topics such as history, programming, news, investigative journalism, and sports. It is similar to the radio, but with better narration and professionalism.

Podcast is a native app that Apple provides for iPad users. You can search a massive library of different podcasts from various sources right from this application. Most of the podcasts that are available in the app are free.

How to Discover New Podcasts

1. To discover and listen to different podcasts, tap on the Podcasts application on the home screen.

2. Once the application is opened, you can go to the bottom of the screen and tap on the "Browse" tab to see featured podcasts selected by the Apple algorithm. Some popular podcasts loved by the Apple curation team will also be displayed in the browse section. If you want to listen to some trending podcasts, select one of them and listen.

3. You can go to the bottom of the Browse tab in the application and select "Browse categories" options to choose podcasts based on a category. There are several categories such as health, news, comedy, music, education,

and history for you to choose from. When you click on a specific category, the podcasts related to that category appear for you to either subscribe or listen to.

4. You can also use the search button to find your favorite podcasts based on the keyword provided.

Once subscribed to any podcasts, the application will automatically notify you whenever a new episode is released. Just click on the notification to start listening to these podcasts. In the more recent versions of iPad OS, it is also possible to look at the transcripts related to these podcasts.

CHAPTER 10:
Accessibilities on Your iPad

iPads are fantastic devices even for people with physical disabilities. No other tablets in the market provide features for supporting people with vision, motor, hearing, and physical disabilities.

It is also straightforward to configure these accessibility features within just a few steps.

The iPad provides an easy way to set them up for users to start using accessibility features right from the device setup.

• Just after switching on the power button, you can triple-click the home button or top button (iPad Pros) three times to turn on Voiceover.

• Just after switching on the power button, you can double-tap the screen with three fingers to turn on the Zoom accessibility feature.

• You can also set other accessibility features right after selecting the language and country.

However, if you want to set up accessibility settings after setting up the iPad, go to Settings>Accessibility to choose one of the many features mentioned below.

Apple divides its Accessibility features into different types based on the impairment.

We will be looking at some of the essential accessibility features of the iPadOS for the users.

VoiceOver

VoiceOver is a screen reader that works with gestures.
Whenever you tap the screen, it will provide audible descriptions for the device owner to easily interact with the device. You can easily change the pitch and speaking rate according to your needs in the settings. VoiceOver is a great accessibility feature for people with visual disabilities.

You can use Siri to activate VoiceOver with the command:. "Hey, Siri! Turn on VoiceOver."

Alternatively, you can go to Settings>Accessibility>VoiceOver and then either turn on or off using the option.

Tap, double-tap, t, and swipe left, right, up, and down are some of the gestures that you need to practice for quicker movement while accessing your device.

How to Change VoiceOver Settings

Apple makes sure that visually impaired people can use the iPad without any problem, hence there are a lot of settings that can help you use the device without any issues.

1. Audio Options
When the voiceover happens, you can use

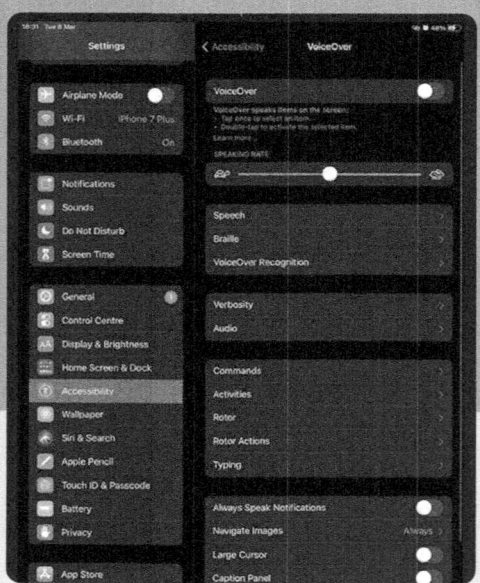

the volume buttons to increase or decrease the volume. You can head over to Settings>Accessibility>VoiceOver>Audio to change some of the audio options provided. You can adjust sound effects and route audio to external audio devices such as amplifiers from these options.

2. VoiceOver Language

VoiceOver language pronunciation usually depends on the language and region you have chosen while setting up. You can go to Settings>General>Language & Region to change your default voiceover language at any time.

3. Speaking Voice

You can adjust the speaking rate in the same tab. Choose a voice from the different voices available, and adjust the pitch by dragging the slider. If you want to include your own pronunciations, go to Speech>Pronunciations, add a new phrase, and dictate it using the "+" word.

To get the most out of the VoiceOver feature, you must learn some VoiceOver gestures. These gestures help you to move around the screen quickly and control them.

Some examples of VoiceOver gestures:

- **Tap the item** - To select and speak an item
- **Swipe right** - To select the next item
- **Two-finger swipe right** - To move into a group of items
- **Swipe left** - To select the previous item
- **Two-finger swipe left** - To move out of a group of items
- **Four-finger tap on the top of the screen** - To select the first item near the top of the screen
- **Four-finger tap on the bottom of the screen** - To select the first item near the bottom of the screen
- **Two-finger tap on the screen** - Pause or resume speaking

- **Three-finger tap on the screen** - Speak additional text such as "alt" text that +describes images

While these are the basic gestures, there are many advanced options that you can practice in the VoiceOver settings tab to get familiar with the different accessibility options provided. No other operating system offers a wide variety of options like iOS provides for visually disabled users.

Screen Zoom

Zoom is one of the specific accessibility features available for all iPad users.
Apart from native apps, many third-party applications from the App Store also provide easy ways to zoom in or out on specific items. You can zoom in on photos or sometimes on the whole screen while using the voiceover mode.

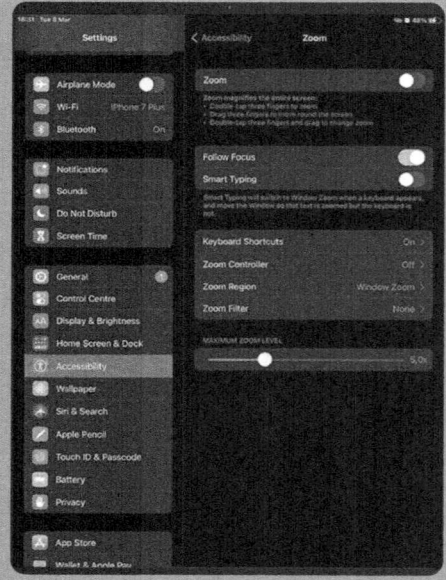

To activate Zoom, go to Settings>Accessibility>Zoom and use the options to either turn on or off the Zoom feature. To use Zoom, all you have to do is double-tap the screen with three fingers.

When you open Settings>Accessibility>Zoom, several settings such as Zoom Pan, Zoom Filter, and Follow Focus can be customized to enhance your Zoom experience.

Display & Text Size

People with color blindness and vision challenges can use Display & Text Size options to enhance their device UI.
This alternative UI can help them use the screen more efficiently.
Go to Settings>Accessibility>Display & Text Size to access these settings. You can adjust any of the following settings mentioned.

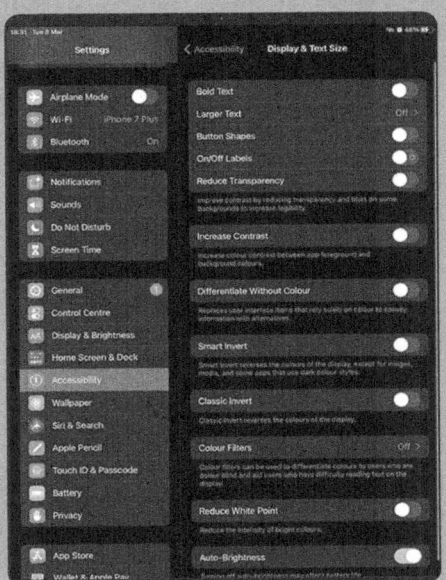

- **Bold Text** - Makes all the characters on the screen become boldface characters.

- **Larger Text** - Provides you a slider to increase the size of the characters on the screen.

- **Button Shaper** - This accessibility option creates an underline for the areas where you can tap.

- **Reduce Transparency** - This option makes it easy to blur some noisy backgrounds.

- **Increase Contrast** - This option increases the contrast of the characters and makes it easy for the characters to read.

- **Auto-Brightness** - Using the built-in ambient light sensor, the device will automatically adjust the screen brightness according to your surroundings.

- **Smart Invert** - This option will reverse the colors making it easy for people with a partial vision to read characters

Once options are set, your device will be auto-adjusted to the new settings provided.

Spoken Content and Descriptions

Even if the user turns the voice off, they can make their iPad read the selected text or even the entire screen with just a click using the Speech Settings.

Head over to Settings>Accessibility>Spoken Content and adjust different options available to make it possible.

● By toggling on the Speak Selection button, you can hear the selected text using the Speak button.

● By toggling on the Speak Screen button, you can hear the entire screen by swiping down with two fingers from the top of the screen.

● By selecting the Voices button, you can change the default voice packs for different languages.

● You can also change the speaking voice by dragging the slider that is present.

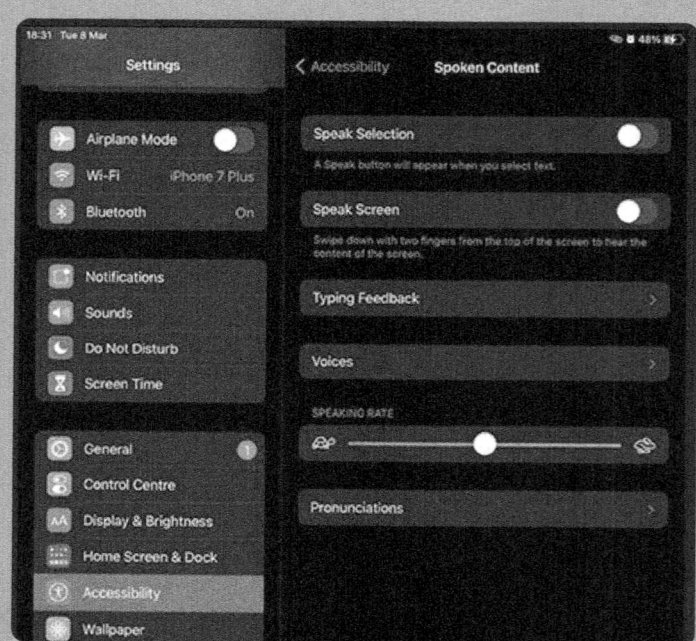

You can also play audio descriptions if they present any video content that is playing.

To ensure that the iPad detects this option, you need to turn on the Audio Descriptions options present in Settings>Accessibility>Audio Descriptions.

Assistive Touch

While the above accessibility options primarily focus on providing a better experience for people with visual problems, Assistive Touch focuses on making the lives better for people with Physical and Motor issues. Assistive touch was initially a smart Accessibility option present in iPhones that were later adapted for iPads.

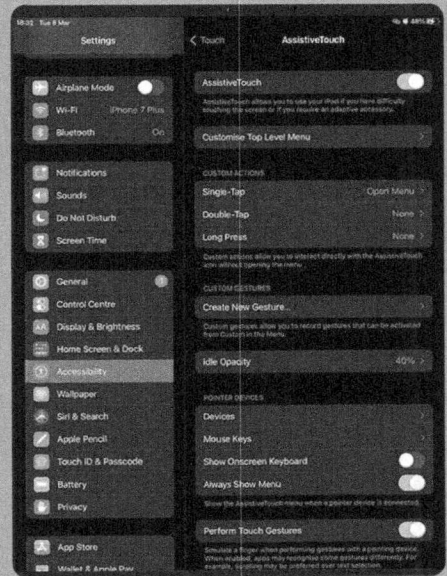

The primary purpose of Assistive touch is not to let the user touch the home or top button if they have any motor problems. To turn on Assistive touch, head over to Settings > Accessibility > Touch > Assistive Touch and Turn it on.

A slight touch control will now appear on the screen. Just click on it anytime, and a new set of commands will be presented for you to select. You can customize all these assistive touch controls from the Assistive Touch menu.

There are many default gestures, but you can also customize new gestures by going to Settings > Accessibility > Touch > Assistive Touch and Clicking on Create new gesture.

Voice Control

Apple makes it easy to control your iPad with just voice commands. It may become handy when you cannot touch the iPad for any reason.

Head over to Settings>Accessibility and click on Voice Control to set-up voice control. For the default commands to work, you must first download a file from this menu.

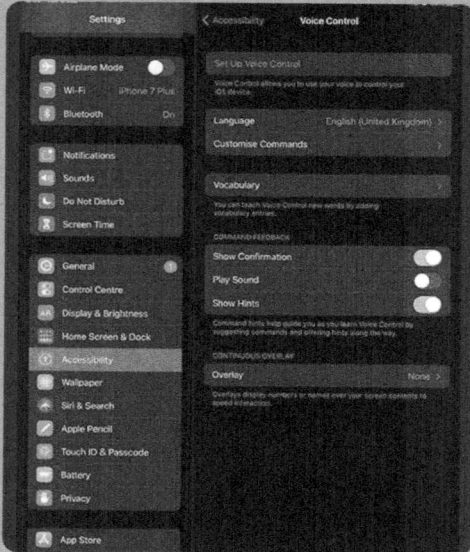

Once the file is downloaded, you can set a different language, vocabulary, and overlay options in this section. Once everything is set up, turn on the Voice control option.

Here are some of the example voice control commands:

- Open control center
- Go to home screen
- Click on Safari
- Turn off the iPad
- Take screenshot
- Tap Stocks

Background Sounds

While this is not precisely an accessibility feature, it can help you focus better when working or while trying to meditate.

These background sounds will play all the time while your iPad is running.

To turn the Background sounds option on or off , you can head over to Settings>Accessibility>Audio & Visual>Background Sounds.

What Can You Choose?

- You can choose a sound from the default sound options.

- You can select the volume for these background sounds using the slider present.

- You can select whether or not to play the music when the iPad is locked.

Subtitles and Captions

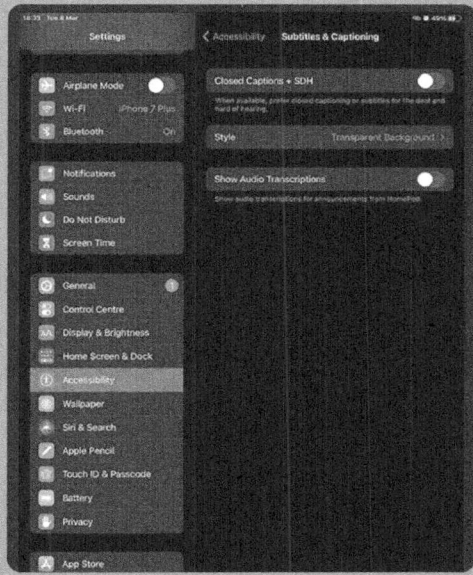

Subtitles and captions are great accessories for people with any hearing issues. iPad always shows standard subtitles and captions available for the reader. However, some media have specially written Subtitles for Hearing Impaired (SDH) for their viewers.

To take a look at any of these subtitles and captions while watching videos, you can click on the icon that looks like a bubble on your media player. You can also customize how these subtitles look from Settings>Accessibility>Subtitles & Captioning.

Once you are in the menu, you can tap on "Style" to change the font, size, color of the captions, and subtitles displayed with the media.

LED Flash for Alerts

You can't keep your ring and notification tones set to make sound all of the time (for example, while watching a movie in a theater).

In these particular circumstances, you can use the LED flash alerts function on your iPad to be aware of different alerts. Also, remember that LED flash alerts will work only when your iPad is locked.

To activate this feature, head over to Settings>Accessibility>Audio & Visual and turn LED Flash for alerts.

Sound Recognition

Your iPad can constantly listen to the different sounds around you and notify you whenever you want.
For example, an iPad can alert you whenever a baby's voice is nearby.
This feature can help you, especially during emergencies.

Head over to Settings>Accessibility>Sound Recognition and click on the "Switch On" option to turn it on.

Once turned on, click on the "Sounds" option and provide the sounds you want your iPad to recognize.

Note: This is just an experimental feature; don't wholly depend on it to recognize voices around your surroundings.

Guided Access

Guided Access helps you focus on a particular task or an app without being distracted by the other features that your device provides.

For example, you can disable the iPad hardware buttons when Guided Access is switched on for a particular app. Get creative with this feature provided by Apple to increase your productivity.

How to Set Up Guided Access

Head over to Settings>Accessibility>Guided Access and switch it on.

In this section, you can set a passcode that you can later use to exit from the Guided Access feature. You can also select Accessibility Shortcuts in this option to quickly turn a Guided Access session on or off.

Step-by-Step Instructions

- To start a Guided Access session, first open an app of your choice.

- Now, when in the app, use the accessibility shortcut or click three times on the Home or top button for the Guided Access session to start.

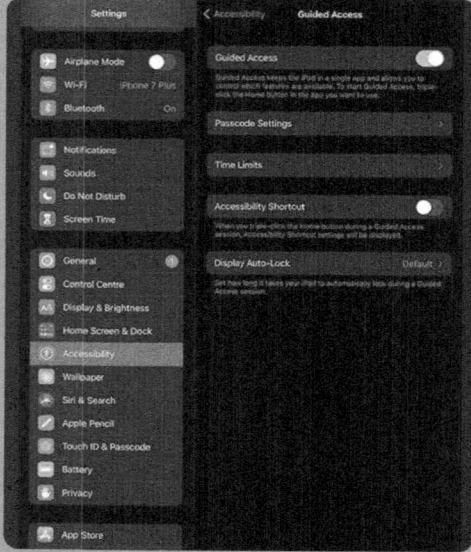

• You can now not exit the app even when you touch the hardware buttons. To exit Guided Access mode, click on the Home button two times, and enter the passcode you set up before. This will end the Guided Access session.

Apart from the general accessibility settings you have learned in this chapter, you can also set settings for every app available in the App Store. Head over to Settings>Applications and browse the Accessibility options to add unique settings for each of them.

Location Sharing

iPad provides an easy way to share your current location with your family members or friends.
You can also track others' locations if they decide to share their location details with you.

Like every feature, whether or not you need to share your location information is your choice. iPad uses unique Global Positioning System (GPS) networks, Wi-Fi networks, and Location Services to determine where you are located. You can also provide location information access to other apps if you so choose.

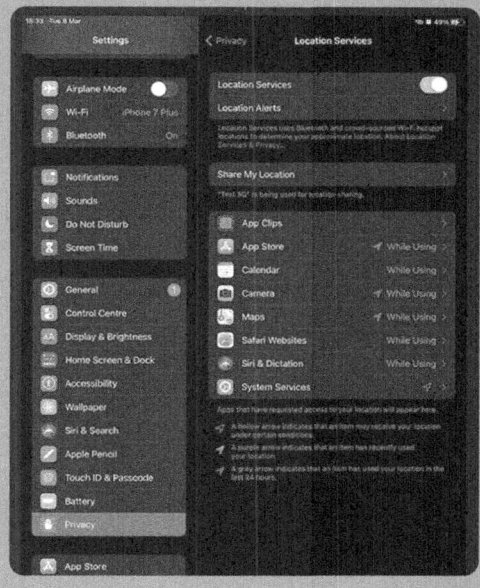

To turn on location services, head over to Settings>Privacy and tap on the location services button.

You will now have an option to toggle the services on. From iPad OS15, you can also directly change the Location Service information on a per-app basis on the same interface. Just click on the app and select how the iPad should provide location services.

You need to be aware of four options while sharing your location with different apps.

● **Never** - When you select this option, that particular app will not be able to access your location in any way.

● **Ask next time or when I share** - When you select this option, iPad will give a pop-up to you whenever the app is trying to access location information.

● **While using the app** - When you select this option, the iPad will be able to access your location only when you are using the app.

● **Precise location** - You need to toggle this option on if you want to provide the precise location of your device. If not toggled, an approximate location will be provided to the app.

You can also look at how default applications and system services will be accessing your location information by heading over to Settings>Privacy>Location Services>System Services.
It is, however, not recommended to change these settings for a better experience with your iPad.

CHAPTER 11:
iPad Accessories

The Apple Ecosystem provides different accessories to expand your iPad to a personal computer level quickly.

With every new update, iPad OS is becoming efficient enough to support new accessories released by both Apple and third-party companies. Knowing how to easily connect these accessories to your iPad device is essential for device owners.

Airpods and Earpods

Airpods have become one of the essential accessories for Apple devices in the past few years. **They are typically headphones but with wireless technology. Airpods provide high-quality sound and a flawless microphone that can make calls. They connect to your device using Bluetooth technology.**

To connect to Airpods from your device, head over to Settings>Bluetooth and turn on the Bluetooth. Without Bluetooth, it is not possible to connect your Airpods.

Now, head over to the home screen and open your Airpods case for the iPad to detect your Airpods automatically. A graphic pop-up will appear on your home screen. Click on the "Connect" button on this pop-up to automatically pair Airpods to your iPad.

If you don't have Airpods, you can also use earpods that come with a headphone jack or lightning connector to listen to music.

All you have to do is insert your earpods connector into the slot to make the iPad use it as output.

Apple Pencil

Apple Pencil is an advanced stylus developed for iPad by Apple.
Apple Pencil is fast and accurate and will instantly work with different iPad models. It is essential to know the two types of Apple Pencil models are available for iPad users. The newer iPad models can support the second generation Apple Pencil, whereas the older iPad models (older than 2018) are only supported for the first generation Apple Pencil.

Apple Pencil comes with palm-rejection technology and makes it easy for digital artists to draw on the iPad screen without worrying about any problems that may otherwise be caused by losing tint control. Apart from professionals, normal users can also use Apple Pencil to take notes, annotate documents, and browse the iPad.

How to Pair Apple Pencil to Your iPad

Ensure that your iPad is unlocked before trying to pair the Apple Pencil with your iPad. If locked, the iPad cannot detect the Apple Pencil. There are two main ways to pair with the Apple Pencil depending on the version of the Apple Pencil you are using.

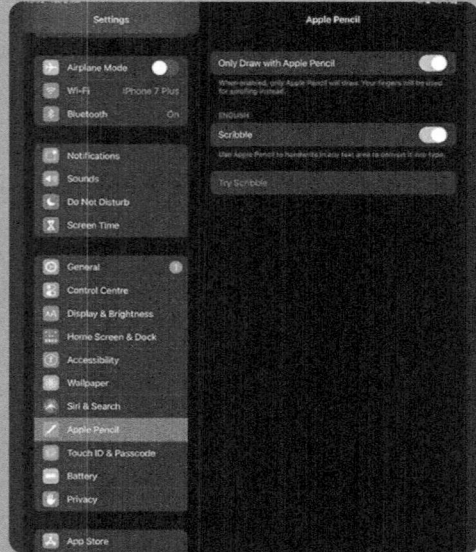

1. If it is the first generation Apple Pencil, uncap the pencil and plug it into the new iPad. A Bluetooth pairing request will pop up within a few seconds, and click on "Pair" for the Apple Pencil to be paired.

2. If it is a second-generation Apple Pencil, then place the Apple Pencil on the magnetic strip present on the iPad to be detected by the device. Once the pop-up comes up, click on "Pair" to connect the device.

Once the Apple Pencil is connected, you can do many incredible things, such as drawing and sketching using premium apps like Procreate, or just entering text in the Notes app or while messaging using the Scribble feature.

How to Use Scribble

To use Scribble, head over to any text field and write with your Apple Pencil in this field. The iPad will automatically detect your handwriting and convert your written text into typed text. You can use the "undo" button to erase any written text or shift into the typed text format by using the keyboard feature.

You can use the pencil icon in the Notes app to shift into an interface that automatically activates the Scribble feature. In the Notes app, you can also tap on the pen icon to change the text color and size of the lines that are being written. Premium apps like GoodNotes, Procreate, and Notability provide additional features for users.

Quick Note Feature

From iPad OS15, you can use the Quick Note feature provided to make notes by swiping up from the bottom right of the screen using an Apple Pencil. The note will be automatically saved to the Notes app. You can draw or scribble with the Quick Note feature.

Apple Keyboard (Magic Keyboard and Smart Folio)

For an iPad to become an alternative to a personal computer, a keyboard and mouse are a must. Fortunately, Apple has constantly focused on improving different keyboard and mouse support for different iPad models. There are also several third-party wireless Bluetooth keyboards and mice connected to your iPad.

Apple provides three different keyboard models for other iPad model users.

Magic Keyboard for iPad

This is the newest and the most efficient keyboard for an iPad on the market. The Magic Keyboard also comes with an inbuilt trackpad making it one of the most valuable accessories available in the Ecosystem.

You can connect your iPad Pro magnetically to the case provided with the Magic Keyboard. You can also change your viewing angles easily with the Magic Keyboard, and quickly charge an iPad by charging the keyboard, as Apple has made it possible to charge your iPad by plugging into the keyboard itself.

To connect to the Magic Keyboard, ensure that your Bluetooth is switched on. Head over to Settings>Bluetooth and click on the Magic Keyboard icon to pair it with the device.

To adjust the keyboard brightness during low-light conditions, you can head over to Settings>General>Keyboard>Hardware Keyboard and drag the slider according to your requirements.

Smart Keyboard Folio for iPad

Not all iPad models support Magic Keyboard. For iPad Air and basic iPad models, Apple provides an alternative with the Smart Keyboard Folio.
It works just as well as the Magic Keyboard, but comes without a trackpad.
To connect to the Smart Folio Keyboard, ensure that your Bluetooth is switched on. Head over to Settings > Bluetooth and click on the Smart folio keyboard to pair it with the device.

Apple Mouse and Trackpad

For a complete office setup having a trackpad along with a keyboard is essential. Apple provides excellent trackpads for all iPad models.

To connect to your Magic Trackpad, make sure it is charged and powered on. Head over to Settings, switch on the Bluetooth, and search for new devices to pair it to the device.

Some Gestures for Magic Trackpad:

● To click, press once on the trackpad.

● To hold, press once on the trackpad and hold with one finger.

● To drag and move, click once on the trackpad and hold it while sliding it with your finger.

● Tap once on the Magic Keyboard for it to wake if it is in a locked state.

● With one finger, swipe to the bottom of the screen to go to the home screen from any application.

● To open the control center, swipe with your hand to the top right.

● To open the notification center, swipe with your hand to the top left .

● To switch between apps, swipe either left or right with three fingers.

● To zoom in on any images or maps, use the pinch gesture with your fingers.

While the trackpad provides more gestures for iPad users, you can still use a regular wireless mouse to do a lot of tasks on your iPad.

To connect to a mouse for iPad, head over to Settings>Bluetooth and connect to the mouse.

Once connected, you can easily control your iPad using gestures such as click and double-click.

Apart from these official accessories from Apple, you can also connect to third-party accessories such as wireless headphones and controllers using the Bluetooth option available in Settings.

CHAPTER 12:
iPad Settings

For any electronic device, customization and personalization are possible with the help of the Settings option.

From computers to handheld consoles, every system makes sure that they provide enough in a Settings interface to access the system according to their wish.

While the Apple Ecosystem restricts you from accessing system files in any way, it provides an excellent Settings menu for the users to solve most of their problems.

If you want to get the most out of your iPad or have a basic understanding while troubleshooting your problems, you need to be aware of the Settings menu and several tasks that it can perform.

First of all, make sure that you are connected to your Apple ID and iCloud, as mentioned in the previous chapters, to get the most out of this chapter as many settings are interlinked with Apple ID and iCloud to work.

Click on the Settings app on the home screen to immediately open an interface divided into two sections.

The first section is the main settings menu, whereas the second section reflects the content of the option we have selected in the first section.

The settings menu is divided into eight separate individual sections.

At the top left of the screen, a search option is provided to quickly search from the many settings options available for the user.

Apple ID & iCloud Settings

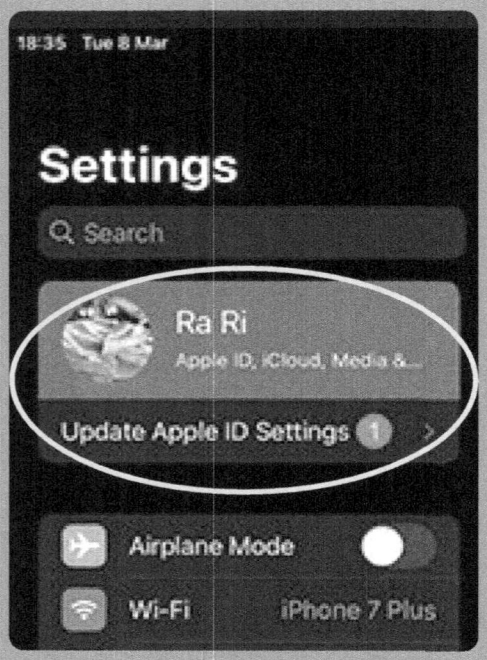

The first section in the Settings menu is related to your Apple ID and iCloud details.

● You can change the personalized details such as profile picture, name of the Apple ID owner, date of birth, email address, and phone number related to your Apple ID from this section. Apple may ask you to confirm your Apple ID passcode for some changes.

● From the Password & Security section you can change your password or switch two-factor authentication for your iPad on or off. It is always recommended to switch on two-factor authentication for your device.

● In the Payment & Shipping option you can change the default payment details that you have provided for Apple services.

In the Subscription' section you can look at your current live app subscriptions and Apple services.
You can also look at your iCloud storage details from this section. You can click on the iCloud option to check which apps use most of your iCloud storage space. By clicking on the "Manage Storage" button you can also delete any unuseful data present in the drive. Make sure to reconfirm your decision before deleting this data because the deleted data cannot be recovered in any way from the cloud servers.

You can also perform the Find My iPad and Family Sharing options previously discussed in this section.

Network and Connection Settings

The second section in the Settings menu is usually about the network settings.

You can connect to your Wi-Fi from here. If you have a cellular iPad, then there will be an option to create a portable hotspot from your device for others to use. You can click on the "i" button beside Wi-Fi access points to configure different settings for the access point.

If you are on a cellular iPad, you can select the mobile network from this section. There is also an Airplane Mode option to toggle your Wi-Fi and mobile networks quickly on or off . Airplane Mode is recommended when you have less battery and want to avoid any connections that can drain your battery.

Apart from network connections, you can also access Bluetooth settings from this section. You can quickly toggle Bluetooth on or off from this section.

Whenever a new device can be paired with your device, it will appear below the "Other Devices" option. All of your paired devices will appear above this option. You can click on the "i" button beside the connected Bluetooth devices to unlink them with your device.

The final option in this section will be Virtual Private Network (VPN).

VPNs are essential, especially if you need to access a local network. To access the VPN network, you first need to add a VPN configuration file from the app. Once the configuration file is added, you can easily connect or disconnect them from this section.

iPad Utility and Productivity Settings

iPad provides different settings related to notifications, sound, display, and Screen Time to make your time with the iPad as seamless and productive as possible.

Notification Settings

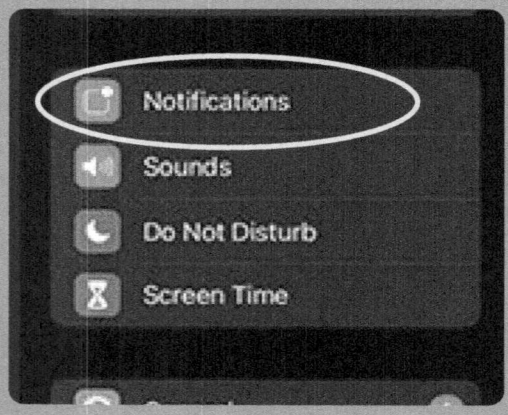

Notifications help you to get immediate alerts from your favorite people and apps.

Notifications, however, can be distracting, especially if you want to have a productive day with your iPad. iPad OS provides an easy way to handle notifications for different applications using the per-app menu.

Head over to Settings>Notifications and click on any app of your choice to understand how notification settings work on your iPad.

After tapping on the app, you will be taken to a new interface with a toggle ON/OFF option to display notifications. If you toggle the button off , then the notifications for this particular application will be disabled.

If you toggle the notifications options on, several other alternatives will be displayed for you on the interface.

You can choose where to display your alerts

- Lock Screen
- Notification Center
- Banners

It is entirely your choice which of the following options you need. You can also select the banner style as temporary or persistent according to the importance of those notifications.

Tap on the "Sounds" option to choose the sound for your notifications in the same interface. You can only use the default sounds provided by Apple for your notifications.

Sounds

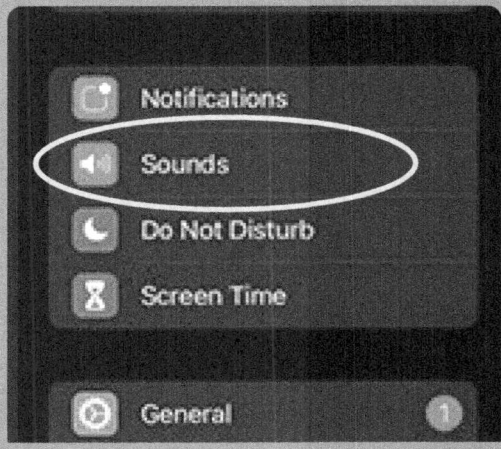

This section helps you customize your sound settings depending on different use cases.

Reduce Loud Sounds
Toggle this option on if you want your device to analyze your listening patterns and automatically reduce your device's sound when you have reached a specific decibel level. If you use headphones a lot of time, selecting this option is vital for not

making your ears hurt.

You can use the slider to adjust the volume for all alerts and rings in the next column. By default, it is in the middle. We recommend you pull the slider as far right as possible if you cannot recognize quiet sounds.

In the next section, you can select sounds for different alerts such as ringtone, text tone, and mail alerts. You can only use default sounds provided by Apple to set your custom tones.

• **Ringtone** - You can use it if you want a new tone for calls.

• **Text tone** - You can use it if you want a new tone for message alerts.

• **New mail** - You can use it if you want a new tone for received mails.

• **Calendar alerts** - You can use it if you want to set a new notification tone for calendar alerts.

• **Airdrop** - You can use it if you want to get a notification tone once the Airdropped files are sent

Focus

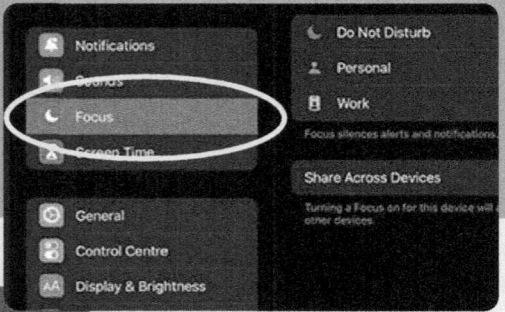

Focus and ScreenTime help you restrict your usage for a temporary amount of time depending on your chosen options.

The iPad is highly addictive and can sometimes make you waste a lot of time without doing any productive work.

With these options, you can now use the device only when necessary. Focus settings help you to allow only a few notifications that are extremely important to you.

By default, there are three modes available for the iPad user:"Do Not Disturb," "Personal," and "Work."

How to Create Your New Focus

- To create your own "Focus," head on over to Settings>Focus and click on the "+" button.

- A new pop-up will arise where you need to choose a type of focus. "Fitness," "Gaming," and "Reading" are some of the default options. You can also select the custom option to create a new name for the focus. After selection, click on the "Next" button to customize your focus.

- In the first interface, you will be able to use the "Allowed People" option to select specific contacts you want to get notifications from while this focus is on.

- You can also select the "Calls From" option to choose a group of contacts such as "Favorites" from your contacts. Once selected, click on the "Allow" button to proceed to the next section.

- In this section you will be able to select apps that you want to receive notifications from when your focus is on. Click on the "Add" button to select an app from your app library. Toggle The 'Time Sensitive" option to not receive notifications from other apps.

• Click on the "Allow" option for your focus to be created. You can now click on the "Done" button to head back to Focus settings.

You can start a customized focus directly from the Control Center, or go to Settings>Focus and toggle your customized focus on.

iPad General Settings

This section helps you change different settings related to Apple iPad to improve your experience with the device.

General Settings

Click on Settings>General to access a wide variety of options to provide more information about your device.

• You can click on "About" to know your device's name, software version, and model number. You can also see whether your device is under warranty from this section.

● By clicking on "Software Update" you will be able to upgrade your device.

● You can click on "Airdrop" to change some default settings for that function.

● You can click on "Airplay" to toggle the option to connect your media to nearby TV's automatically on.

● You can toggle the "Picture-in-Picture" option on to play media files, even when you press the home button on an overlay.

● By clicking on the "iPad Storage" option, you can check how much memory your apps are using.

If you want to delete any data related to an app from this section, tap on the app and click on the "Delete data" button. Remember that all of the data will be permanently deleted, so be careful before performing this task.

● Tap on the "Background App Refresh" button to decide which app(s) you want to refresh.

● You can change the date and time displayed on your device.

● You can change the keyboard that you are using, and can add any shortcuts for your text keyboard.

● You can click on fonts to add customized fonts for your device. Usually, you need to install font apps from the App Store first to utilize this feature.

● Click on "Language & Region" to change the language and location of your device.

Control Center Settings

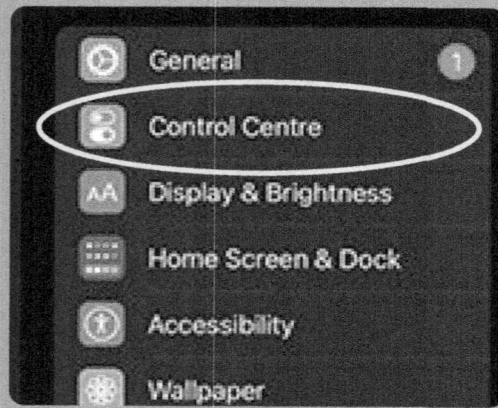

\Control Center helps users easily interact with different features that the device provides with just a down-swipe. You can customize how your Control Center should look from Settings>Control Center.

First, toggle the button beside "Access Within Apps" on if you want to access the Control Center from the app itself.

If not, it is toggled on, and you may need to be on the home screen to access the Control Center.

In the next section you will see different options that are already present in your Control Center. Just click on the "-" icon beside them to delete any of them from the Control Center. You can also click on the three horizontal lines to rearrange the controls.

In the next section, you can add different controls to your Control Center. There are many controls for you to choose from. Click on the "+" button beside them to add them to your Control Center.

Some important controls to choose:

- Alarm
- Camera
- Low-Power Mode
- Screen Recorder
- Dark Mode
- Accessibility Shortcuts
- Stopwatch

Display and Brightness

In this section, you can control different options that can help you personalize your screen display.

- Select whether you want to choose Light or Dark Mode.

- Use the slider on the screen to increase or decrease the screen's brightness.

- You can switch Night Shift on or off ,that can help you to provide a warmer screen.

- You can customize the Auto-lock feature according to your usage for better security and for saving your battery.

- You can increase or decrease the text size.

- You can bold the text.

Home Screen & Dock

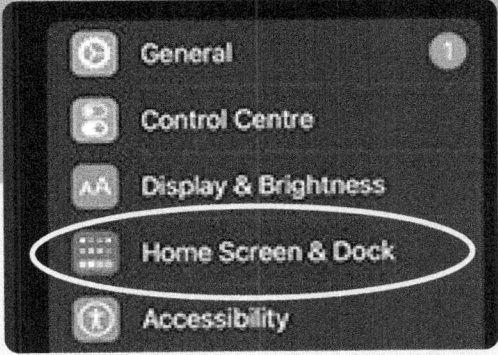

In this section, you can customize your home screen and dock settings.

Just select the appropriate options according to your preference for better customization.

- You can choose whether or not to use large app icons.

- You can choose whether or not to show the app library in the dock.

Battery Settings

This section helps you understand more about your battery's performance and different statistics related to it.

- You can toggle the battery percentage option on to display your current charge percentage.

- You can activate Low-power mode You can also look at how much battery a specific app has used in this section.

Privacy Settings

This section provides a clear view for the user about what applications

ask for information about your contact details, file information, and speech-related queries.

Just clicking on the app and conducting a review can help you decide which apps are unsafe for your device.

App Store and Wallet Settings

Tap on the "App Store" button to quickly adjust some settings related to updates and automatic downloads of app updates.

There is also an option to stop getting prompts that developers ask you to provide reviews and ratings for their app.

You can tap on the "Wallet" option in the same section to quickly look at the cards you have added to your iPad wallet.

You can add a new card by tapping on the "Add Card" button. It is also easy to delete these cards by clicking on the "Edit" button and pressing on "-."

Default Native App Settings

In this section, you will be able to change settings for utility and communications-specific applications present in the iPad, such as Safari, Notes, and Maps.

This section also provides the "Passwords" option to check all of the passwords added to your iCloud Relay.

Just click on the "Passwords" option, and a pop-up will open to enter your passcode.

If your default authentication is by FaceID or TouchID, you also need to provide them for all of the passwords to appear in this section.

You can now click on any password to look at the account details or delete them.

If you did change the password for any of the accounts, you can quickly update the password using the "Edit'" button.

Default Entertainment and Photo App Settings

In the seventh section of the Settings menu, you can change default Apple entertainment applications such as Apple Music, Podcasts, and Game Center.

Third-Party App Settings

In the final section of the Settings menu, you will be able to change settings for the third-party apps you have installed from the App Store.

Developers provide different settings for different apps. Most of the apps include a Privacy Policy, Acknowledgements, and Debug information in this section.

All of the apps in this section have an easy way to customize how Siri interacts with this application. Just click on the "Siri & Search" option present and customize it according to your preference.

CHAPTER 13:
Tricks and Tips for your iPad

The iPad is a wonderful device designed with the focus of providing value to the consumer. Apple made sure to introduce different simple tricks for the user to enrich their experience with this device. In this chapter we will look at some of the tricks that can help you in different situations.

Take a Screenshot

Taking screenshots is an essential skill that all iPad users need to know.

All of the screenshots you take will usually be saved after confirming them, and any unsaved screenshots will automatically be deleted from the internal memory of the iPad.

There are two different ways to take screenshots, depending on the iPad model you are using.

For iPads Without a Home Button

If you are using an iPad without a home button, you need to press the top button and any volume button simultaneously, and then quickly release them to trigger a screenshot of your entire screen.

For iPads With a Home Button

If you are using an iPad with a home button, you need to press the top and home buttons simultaneously, and then quickly release them to trigger a screenshot of your entire screen.

Once your screenshot is done, a small thumbnail will appear on the bottom left of the screen. If you don't click on the thumbnail or swipe it, the screenshot will disappear from your iPad.

What Screenshot Options You Have

When you tap on the thumbnail, you will be taken to an interface where you can apply different options to your screenshot.

● You can increase the transparency of the screenshot by using the slider provided on the top left of the screen.

● You can edit the picture by tapping on the en symbol provided. You can even use an Apple Pencil to make any notes on the image.

• In the picture itself, there is a crop option to select only a part of the screenshot.

Once everything is alright with the screenshot, you can click on Done" to save the screenshot to your photo gallery or files. There is also an option to delete the screenshot, or share the screenshot with other apps.

Dark Mode

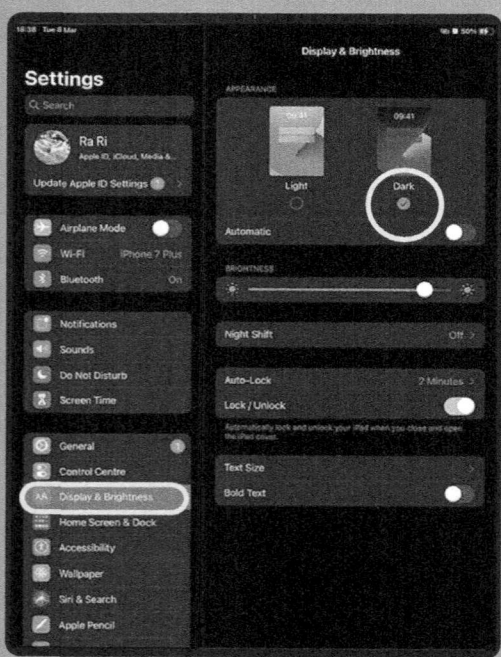

Dark mode is an exclusive system-wide feature introduced in iOS13 for all iOS devices.

Dark mode provides a better experience for users, especially when using the iPad in low-light environments. All of your apps and browsers will change to dark mode when this function is turned on. You can also add this control to the Control Center to quickly change from light to dark mode, or vice versa, within a few seconds. To change to dark mode manually, head over to Settings>Display & Brightness and click on the "Light" or "Dark" option. You can also toggle the "Automatic" option on if you want to automatically change into dark mode after a set time.

Measure App

The Measure app makes it easy to gauge the size of real-world objects with the help of augmented reality technology.

Newer iPad Pro models use Lidar sensors to ensure that the measurements are as accurate as possible.

So how can you take measurements using the Measure app?

Tap on the Measure app from the app library and follow the onscreen instructions carefully.

● The iPad Measure app will usually display a frame of reference on the screen for you to place the surface on it. Keep moving the device until you see a circle with a dot.

● After the dot appears, place it on the item you are trying to measure and tap on the "+" button. You have now registered the starting point.

● Now move the line to the endpoint where you want to measure and click on the "+" button again.

The app will now measure the distance and provide accurate measurements.

Using a rectangle, you can continue the same process to measure other complex systems.

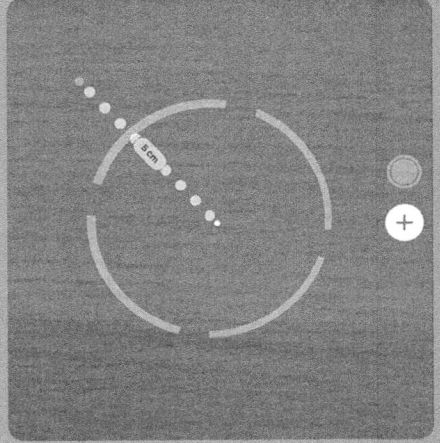

How to Measure a Person's Height Using the Measure App

The newer iPad Pro models have an additional feature of measuring a person's height with the help of portrait mode.

Open the Measure app and ensure that the person whose height you are trying to measure is in the viewfinder. Once detected, the app will automatically calculate the person's height and display it on the screen. For accurate measurements, make sure that there is enough light and no reflective surfaces nearby.

Do Not Disturb Mode

Do Not Disturb mode is one of the classic features in the Apple Ecosystem.

With this mode on, it becomes easy to ignore calls automatically when you are busy.

With iPad OS15, several new features are added in the name of Focus.
Focus helps Apple users customize how they want to use the device in different situations.

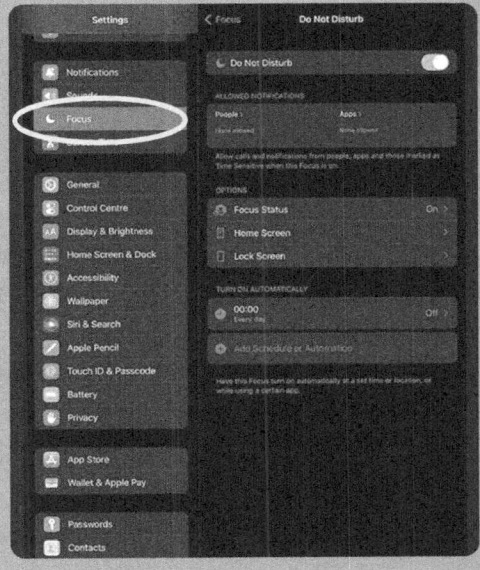

• To use Do Not Disturb mode, you need to customize Focus settings.
To access these settings, head over to Settings>Focus.

• Once in the Focus settings, tap on the Do Not Disturb option.

• You now need to toggle the Do Not Disturb mode on to activate across your device.

• In the settings option, you can add exceptions by adding people and apps that you want to receive notifications from.

• At the end of the options list, you can select a time to activate Do Not Disturb mode automatically.

Group FaceTime

iPads make it easy for users to start a video call with many people at once - even 32 people if you want.
In the pandemic world, where video conferences are essential for companies worldwide, Group FaceTime can be a great alternative to video conference applications such as Zoom.

You can start a Group FaceTime from the FaceTime app or a group conversation in the Messages app. To be a part of Group FaceTime, you need to have at least an iOS version of 12.2.

How to Start a Group FaceTime From the FaceTime App

1. Tap on the FaceTime app on the home screen and click on the "New FaceTime button.

2. In the "To" section add all of the contacts you want to start a Group FaceTime with.

3. After adding all of the contacts, click on the "FaceTime" button with a green background to start a new Group FaceTime.

How to Start a Group FaceTime From the iMessage App

1. Head over to your Messages app and create a group, or visit an existing group conversation.

2. On the top of the screen, you will see a "FaceTime icon.
Tap on it.

3. You can now select whether to create an audio or video call.
Once selected, your Group FaceTime call will start.

How to Join a Group FaceTime Call

Apple made it easy for anyone to join a FaceTime call they have been invited to. Just click on the 'Join" button in the Messages app. If you are in any other app, you will get a call notification, just like with cellular calls. Just click on the notification and tap on "Join" to join your group members in the FaceTime call.

Silence Unknown Callers

Spam calls are annoying and are common these days.
You can restrict these unknown calls to end automatically with the Focus mode. However, you do not need to turn on "Do Not Disturb" mode to silence these unknown callers every time.
From iPad OS13 onwards, Apple has provided a specific option for users to achieve this task quickly. First, head over to Settings>Phone and toggle the option "Silence Unknown callers" on.
With this turned on, you will not receive any calls from numbers you have never contacted. On the other hand, you will receive calls from numbers you have messaged or communicated with before, even if they are not in your contacts.

Energy-Saving Mode

The iOS low-power mode was popular right from its inception in iPhones from iOS9.

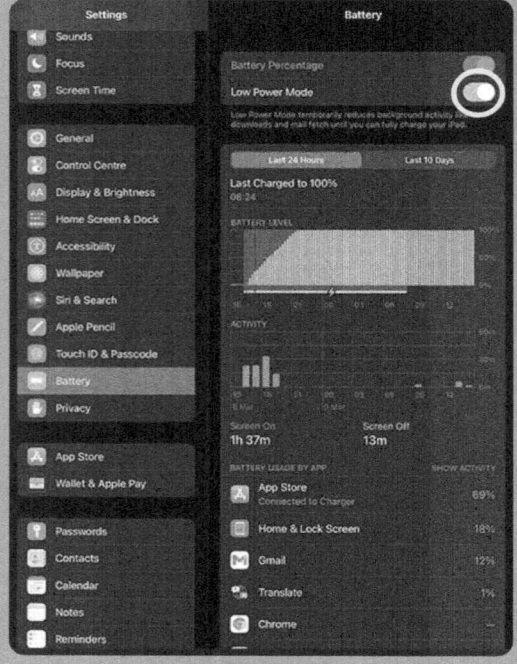

iPads, however, have got this feature only on iOS15.

The energy-saving mode doesn't just decrease screen brightness or background refresh, it also reduces the overclock processing power of the iPads Central Processing Unit (CPU) to get more usage from the device.

To activate energy-saving mode, head over to Settings>Battery and toggle the low-power mode option on.

You can also add it to the Control Center for faster access.

Flash Like a Flashlight

The Camera app usually uses flash to take pictures in low-light backgrounds.

The light-emitting diode (LED) flash present in iPads can also act as a flashlight anytime you want to by just clicking on the flashlight icon in your Control Center.

Holding the flashlight button on the Control Center will also provide you with an option to easily increase or reduce the brightness of the flashlight.

Memojis

Memojis are advanced emojis that Apple created for its messaging platform. You can send these emojis to your contacts in the Messages and FaceTime apps. Memojis match your personality and mimic your facial expressions. To create your own memoji, go to the Messages app and click on the new conversation icon or go to an existing conversation.

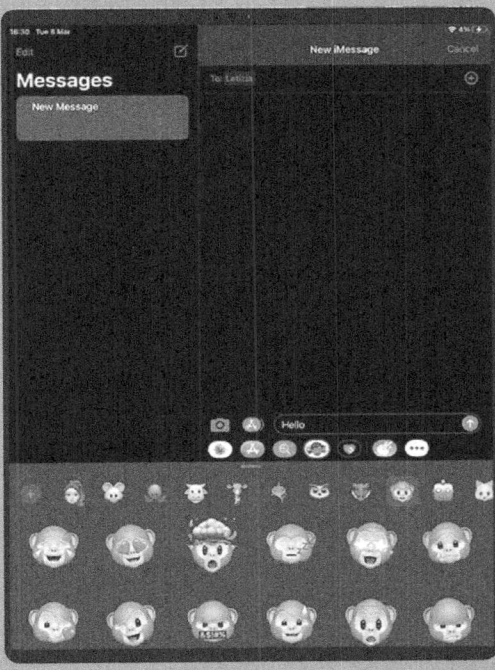

• Once in the conversation, tap on the memoji button (usually third from the left). You will now be able to see all of the default memojis provided by Apple. There are more than 30 memojis for you to choose from.

• Click on the "+" button to create your own memoji and to customize different features such as skin tone, hairstyle, eyes, and a lot more.

• Once everything is set to your liking, tap on the "Done" button to create the memoji. You can now record voice while sending your memoji to mimic your expressions on your customized avatar.

Memoji Stickers

All of your memojis will automatically be converted into sticker apps.

Instead of memoji videos, you can send these sticker apps in messages and other third-party messaging apps like WhatsApp and telegram.

1. Click on the memoji button on the Messages app or any third-party messaging app.

2. Now, select your avatar to look at all of the stickers that are generated for your memoji.

3. Tap on any one of them to send using the blue arrow button.

Animated Memojis

While memoji stickers are great, animated memojis are fun for many users. You can send a whole video with your audio and memoji. However, only new iPad Pro and Air models support this feature. You can use these animated memojis even while taking a FaceTime call.

1. Click on the memoji icon and tap on the record button for the animation to begin.

2. Do anything on the camera, and it will be reflected on the memoji animation.

3. Once done, click on the blue arrow button to send it using the Messages app. Remember that you can't send these animated memojis to third-party apps such as WhatsApp.

Similarly, during a FaceTime video call, click on the "Effects" icon present to use your favorite memoji.

Cut, Copy, and Paste Between iDevices

The advantage of having a well-integrated ecosystem is that you can practically do anything with your devices when connected with the same Apple ID and on the same Wi-Fi network.
For example, you can copy a bunch of text on your iPad and send it to your iPhone.

How to achieve tasks like these?

• Confirm that both devices are connected with the same Apple ID.

• Confirm that both devices are on the same network.

• Confirm that Bluetooth is switched on and that both the devices are near each other for a better Bluetooth connection.

• Now select a bunch of text on iPad and use your fingers to make a pinch gesture. You will now get the option to "Send to iPhone."
Tap on it for the text to be transferred to your iPhone clipboard.

• You can also use this technology to send images or any other attachments.

• Sharing app links will automatically install the app on your other device after authentication.

Portable Printer

All Apple devices use AirPrint to easily print any files or web pages with the help of a modern printer.

AirPrint is integrated with almost every modern printer available now.

How to use it?

• Make sure that your iPad and printer are connected to the same Wi-Fi network for the wireless print functionality to work.

• On any web page or document, click on the share button icon and tap on the "More Options" button.

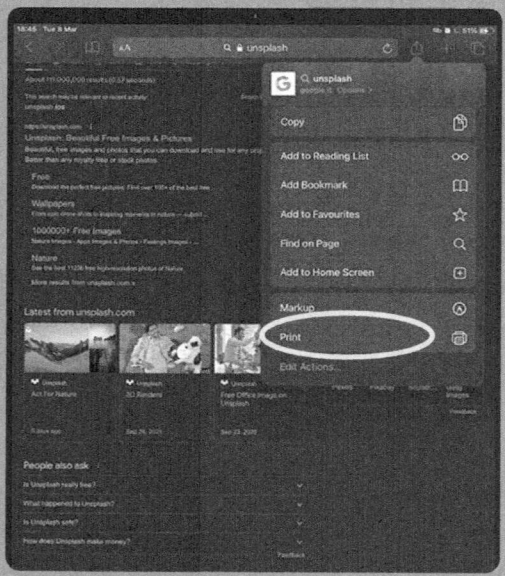

• You will now be able to see a printer icon and tap on it to head to the next interface.

• In this interface, you will have the option to select your printer, how many copies you want to print, and how many pages you want to print if it is a document.

- Once the information is entered, click on the "Print" button on the top right corner to complete the job.

Widgets

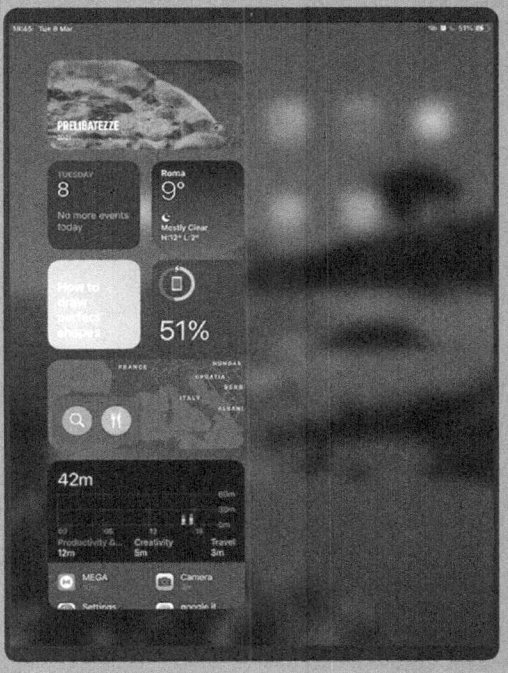

Widgets are a new addition to the Apple Ecosystem.

From iPad OS15, users can use widgets on any part of the screen.

Apple provides several default widgets, and there are already thousands of third-party applications utilizing the widget framework to create widget-centric applications.

The primary purpose of widgets is to provide specific app information on the home screen itself without having to navigate to the app.

For example, if you order a pizza from the Domino's app, you can track that order and how many minutes it will arrive from the widget on your home screen.

On an iPad, you can add widgets to the home screen and a specially-designed interface for the iPad known as 'Today's View."

How to Add Widgets to Your Home Screen

Go to the home screen and touch and hold anywhere that is empty.

After a few seconds, you will enter into editing mode, where you can see a "+" button to the top left of the screen.

• Click on this button for the widget panel to open. You can select any widget from the list on the left.

• When you select a widget from the list, you will then be able to choose different variations of that particular widget. Choose one of these by swiping right or left.

• After deciding, you can click on the "Add Widget" button to add it to the home screen. You can also adjust and reorder your widgets during this process, just like how you can change app icon placement on the home screen.

How to Add Widgets in "Today's View" on iPad

• To go to "Today's View," swipe your finger to the right on the home screen until you see a new interface that is with a column widget list.

• When on this interface, tap and hold on any part of the screen for the editing mode to be enabled.

• Now click on the "+" button to add different widgets to your "Today's View."

You can use advanced widget stacks provided by Apple to include one or more widgets from different apps on the same block.

CONCLUSION

Congratulations on completing the guide. iPads are great devices, and we hope that you will get the most out of your device. If you are a person who gets anxiety while dealing with any new technology, then read the simple tricks below to relieve any anxiety that can occur.

Tricks to Relieve Anxiety While Using Technology

1. Always Google
If you are confused about any feature that you are not aware of, feel free to search the term using Google.
There will always be a ton of articles written for you to understand these simple tasks.

2. Read the Apple Official Guide
Apple provides comprehensive guides for all of their devices. You can usually find an app called "Get Started" that describes all of these small functions with a simple guide.
You can also visit Apple's official website to look at these guides.

3. Make Use of YouTube
YouTube is a great resource to follow video guides that can help you troubleshoot your device easily. Just download the YouTube app from the App Store and search for videos that can solve your problem.
Look at the comments before watching the videos because some videos may not be legitimate.

4. Use Apple Support

Apple provides two years of Apple Support for all of their users. All you have to do is open your iMessage app and send your query to the Apple support team. Someone will reply to a query as soon as they see it.

We wish you all the fun with your iPad.

GLOSSARY

Apple ID - Apple ID is the only account that you need to access different services offered by Apple on their devices.

Accessibilities - System Settings that can help users interact with the device easily.

Accessories - Third-party or first-party devices that can help iPad users to maximize their performance and productivity with the device.

AirDrop - An Apple device-specific feature that can be used to share files between different Apple devices easily.

AppStore - The default shop where Apple users can download applications for their iPad or iPhone.

Apple Music - The music subscription that Apple provides for users worldwide.

Backups - A particular file that can be used to restore your iPad from anytime.

Bluetooth - A wireless connection service that can be used to connect accessories to the iPad.

Books - A default application that provides the ability to read books on your iPad in ePub and PDF formats.

Clock - A default application that can be used to keep alarms or to check the world clock.

Calendar - A default iPad application that will help you to create events and manage reminders.

Control Center - An iOS utility that helps you to easily control different inbuilt controls provided by the device, such as Torch, low power mode, and Dark mode.

Do not disturb - Helps you to ignore calls that are not coming from your contacts list.

Dock - Helps you to manage apps that are frequently used on your iPad.

Face ID - A new authentication procedure for iPad users.

FaceTime - Default video chat application for iPad users.

GPS - Navigation system that is used for location sharing and Apple Maps.

iMessages - A default chat application provided by Apple for its users.

iCloud - The cloud service that Apple users can use to upload their data into encrypted servers constantly.

iPad OS - The name of the operating system that the iPad uses.

Maps - A default application that can be used to access navigation features quickly.

Network connection - A way by which you can connect your device to the internet.

Notification Center - An interface where you can look at your app notifications.

Photos - The default iPad application to look at images and videos.

Shortcuts - A default Apple application that helps iPad users to automate things.

Safari - A default web browser developed by Apple to browse the internet on Apple devices such as iPhone, iPad, and Mac.

REFERENCES

A Beginner's Guide to Safari on the iPhone, iPod, and iPad. (n.d.). Lifewire.

Retrieved February 14, 2022, from https://www.lifewire.com/using-Safari-iphone-browser-2000784

dummies—Learning Made Easy. (n.d.). www.dummies.com.

Retrieved February 14, 2022, from https://www.dummies.com/article/technology/electronics/tablets-e-readers/ipads/for-seniors-use-the-ipad-online-user-guide-205699

Never forget a thing by using the Notes app on your iPhone! (2022, January 24). IMore.

https://www.imore.com/how-create-edit-and-delete-notes-iphone-or-ipad

Provan, D. (2018). iPad in easy steps (2nd ed.). Wiley.

INDEX

Made in the USA
Middletown, DE
27 November 2022

16108400R10104